Changing Your Tune!

The Musician's Handbook for Creating Contemporary Worship

Lynn Hurst

ABINGDON PRESS

Changing Your Tune!
The Musician's Handbook for Creating Contemporary Worship

Copyright © 1999 by Abingdon Press

This book is printed on acid-free, recycled paper.

ISBN 0-687-02297-5

99 00 01 02 03 04 05 06 07 08—10 9 8 7 6 5 4 3 2 1

MANUFACTURED IN THE UNITED STATES OF AMERICA

Contents

Preface

My journey from a classical, traditional church musician to a classical, traditional, contemporary church musician has been a challenging process for the last thirteen years. It was not a journey that I ever intended to take. In fact, when I first began my career as a church musician twenty-three years ago, my plans were *never* to do any music that wasn't the best of the classics. The classics were all that I knew. My bachelor of music degree was in piano performance and my intent was to complete a doctorate and teach on the college level or have a performance career. So, in 1975 when I became a church organist at a United Methodist church in Oklahoma and was faced with playing a Gaither anthem, I was stunned! I grew up in a large church with a very strong classical music program that had nurtured my talents. I did not know that music of the Gaither style existed in the church. I am sure the Oklahoma church choir remembers my vow *never* to play music of this kind. My first important lesson of church music was learned: Never say never!

The true meaning behind this lesson was that God did not intend for all people to like the same music or to worship in the same way. Therefore, if I want to help all the people in a congregation to worship, I must learn to do all styles of music well. (There are no congregations that like only one style of music.) Also, I had to learn that no style of worship is superior to another. As a trained musician, I felt that I was more qualified to work with any style of music than those who had had no training. Yes, that even included those things I thought I could never do, such as play by ear and improvise. For the first ten years of my career, I expanded my repertoire of musical styles only on the piano. I found that certain piano arrangements, if played well, enriched my playing and were even a blessing for me. I began to enjoy a new sound.

When I went back to school to get a master of church music degree, my areas of interest expanded to choral conducting and I had a new desire to train the children in our churches in choral excellence. I felt certain that my career for the future would be in a large church with a fully graded choir program. That dream was realized in 1985 when I was hired at Central United Protestant Church in Richland, Washington as the music associate. My responsibilities were to direct and coordinate children's and youth choirs and to be the assistant organist. What I didn't know was that the organist wanted help with the four services she had to accompany each weekend. Two of the services (Saturday evening and Sunday at 8:30 A.M.) were small services in different settings, accompanied by piano only. The Sunday service at 11:00 A.M. was a traditional sanctuary service accompanied by organ. These three services would be easy for me. But the largest service for this church was the contemporary service in the fellowship hall at 9:15 A.M.

My husband (a minister of youth) and I attended all the worship services during our interview with the church. We were most impressed with the unique contemporary service because of the excitement that was in the air. We had never experienced anything like it. Yet I assumed that I would not be a part of this service because it was not in my realm of expertise. I was wrong. Almost immediately, I was asked to take over on the main keyboard (piano) for this service. The organist, who had played for the service since its inception in 1975, played everything by ear! There was no printed music from which I could play. When I was about to say "never," the organist produced lead sheets (melody and guitar chords) that she had handwritten for me. Thus, I was pushed off the high dive. I found that I could swim, but I was scared to death!

For five years I played lead keyboard (piano) with several guitars and a flute. In 1992 I went to a workshop in California for contemporary worship, led by Ron Kenoly. Was I ever a fish out of water! But I left the workshop with a new resolve to learn what I could in order to stay with the current trends in music. We added two synthesizers, percussion, and electric bass to our contemporary service.

In 1989 I had become the organist for the church, so my career had expanded to include a classical organ/traditional service, small intimate services with piano, and a contemporary service on the synthesizer every week. I would never have believed it twenty-three years ago.

Let me assure you that it is possible, with a lot of work, determination, and a change of attitude, to learn skills that you thought you could never have. I have learned to play anything from a lead sheet, to improvise on the spot, and to play a little by ear when necessary. I am still envious of those who play so beautifully by ear with no effort and I continue to struggle with those skills that do not come so naturally to me. But more important, I try to do it all with the same level of excellence I learned in my piano performance degree. All music to the glory of God deserves that level of excellence.

When my husband and I moved to Munsey Memorial United Methodist Church, Johnson City, Tennessee in 1995, I was offered my greatest challenge yet. This older, traditional, downtown church wanted to begin a contemporary service. Yes, I had been working with a contemporary service for ten years, but I knew nothing about starting one from scratch. I knew what worked and where I would like to take this new service, but how to get there would be another learning experience. I now serve Munsey as associate minister of music, which includes expanding a fully graded children's choir program, and serving as assistant organist as well as the director of contemporary worship. I am very blessed to work with Douglas Grove-DeJarnett and Jane LaPella in the music ministry. Munsey Memorial United Methodist Church began its contemporary worship service in September 1996. It has been an exciting and challenging two and a half years!

Munsey's strength will always be its traditional 11:00 A.M. service. That is our history. But now we have added to that history an alternative worship service of a very different style. The service meets in the fellowship hall at 8:45 A.M. on Sunday—simultaneously with a traditional service in the sanctuary. From its beginning the service was designed for Munsey members who desired an alternative style of worship. This group of people spanned several generations so one specific style of music and worship was not its purpose. The musical basis of the service is contemporary soft rock music with a praise band and singers. The way the message will be experienced in the service is most important. Therefore, the music might be blues one week, jazz another, and so on. The challenge before us has been to look at all components of the worship service each week and to be as creative as possible in order to present an experiential, current message for our world today. If that doesn't spark your creative juices, I don't know what will!

There was no "how to" book to begin this service. I have had to search out information and ask many questions to be sure of what was best for our service. So I offer to you in this book my experiences, information, and ideas. I pray that your journey will be a little easier than mine has been because of this information. May God bless you in your journey to expand your ideas of worship and music ministry.

Introduction

Is your church a mainline Protestant church that seems to be declining in numbers and vitality? Are you beginning to wonder what your church will do when the "dedicated few" are no longer there? Are some of the church's traditions not so meaningful anymore? Is your church strong and maintaining or growing its membership, yet receiving requests for differing styles of worship, Bible studies, and small groups?

If you are a trained church musician working in one of the categories above, you are in good company. This is reality. We church musicians have not been trained or even given much insight in how to deal with the dilemmas in the church today.

What can we do for the church that is losing membership and vitality? How can we add different styles of worship in a strong traditional church without upsetting the apple cart? How do we build upon our traditions with integrity?

Take heart! It can be done, it has been done, it is being done right now. So where do you start? You start with your *heart* (better known as your attitude). After all, your worship, Bible study, faith journey, and so on, are simply attitudes of your heart. Is your attitude the same as it was when you were a child? What is the one thing that has been consistent in your life from birth to now? Change! Nothing around you is the same as it was at your birth. It has been necessary for you to change as you moved forward in time. A lot of that change took place in your heart—in your attitude.

Making a change in worship style is not easy, but a change in heart toward worship is even more difficult. Do you continue to plan worship as you experienced it ten or more years ago? Will the people of today hear God's message through the same patterns of worship that you did? Obviously not, for we are a people of change.

This is a book to help you with the "how to" of a new style of worship. Many of those things that you said you would *never* do in worship are addressed. The "what do I do," "where do I start," and "where do I get help" questions will be covered. With each question you ask, remember to begin with your heart. What is your attitude about this change? Are you willing to jump off the high dive, to be the fish out of water, to search out and try new ideas all for the glory of God? If not, please ask God to change your attitude before you try any changes with God's people! It won't be easy. There will be no visible security net under you, only the gift of faith that God gives you.

As you read this book, remember that the traditions of mainline Protestant worship are the basis upon which each worship service is built. It is not possible to change our history, and it is not advisable to ignore it. We must teach new generations who we are in ways that they will hear. Simply put, we must use new technology to explain our faith stories. The Word will not be changed, our faith stories will not change, and the traditions that can be translated to this generation will not change. It is our job to put these traditions into today's language. We must become as creative as possible in presenting God's Word for today. The great challenge before us is to expand our ways of worshiping, to change our attitudes—or in musician's language—to change our tune.

Getting Started

The suggestions that will be made for a new style of worship are designed for a "believers" worship service. There are many believers in our churches today who do not live the Christian faith because God's Word is not being interpreted in a way they can understand. A "seeker" style worship service (a service for persons who are unfamiliar with the Christian faith and worship traditions) will not be addressed. It is understood though, that all worship services should be seeker friendly. A service that is creative in its approach, relevant to today, and presented in current venues will be understood by all.

Unfortunately, there is no "A-B-C" plan that will work for every church. Ideas are exactly that. You will have to take the new ideas and develop the ones that work for your church. Therefore, do not approach any new idea with the attitude that if it worked for them, it will work for us. God may use that new idea in a very different way for your church. Or, possibly some ideas will not fit God's vision for your church.

Which new ideas should you try? The Author of worship will help you know the unique plan for your church. Each outcome will be different. Even as God created no two people alike, there will be no two worship services alike. If you plan to make changes in your current traditional service or add an alternative style of worship, begin by asking the following important questions:

1. Is it God's will for your church?
2. Is there unanimous staff support for the changes?
3. Is there sufficient congregational support?
4. Is there monetary support?
5. Is a design team in place?
6. Is a director/coordinator in place?

You will need to request input from as many people as possible. Use every means available to survey your congregation. Possible questions could be:

1. Would you attend a worship service of a different style?
2. Would you attend at (possible times for the service)?
3. Would you be willing to help in the following ways?
   - lead worship and/or sing
   - play an instrument

- work with a drama team
- greet/usher
- set up the facility
- be a sound/video technician
- create visual arts (altar, banners)
- coordinate publicity

Gathering information from the congregation and evaluating available resources is a necessary beginning step toward the development of new ideas for worship.

Anything new and different in worship will require more time and effort on your part. This alone has scared off many church musicians, because their job already demands too much time. Yet the rewards to your congregation are beyond measure. As for feeling prepared and capable of handling these changes, forget it! You are a pioneer and need a pioneering spirit. Who better to pioneer the changes in worship than those of us who have been trained to facilitate worship? Let's not turn our backs on what is unfamiliar and uncomfortable. If we do the ball we dropped will be picked up by those who know little about planning worship. Instead, be open to new ideas that will stretch you beyond your boundaries of comfort. In so doing, I believe you will experience exciting, meaningful worship!

PART 1

NECESSARY COMPONENTS OF CONTEMPORARY WORSHIP

Chapter 1
The Worship Space

Creating a New "Holy" Space

Any new worship service or change in worship style requires a well-planned worship space. To begin a new service that has a totally different style from your current traditional service, it is advisable, if possible, to create a new worship space in a room other than the sanctuary. People will not have the same expectations that are found in a traditional sanctuary setting if a more relaxed setting is used. A room such as a fellowship hall or large classroom will lend itself to new venues that might not be possible in the traditional sanctuary (e.g., drama, dance, and video). When a formal sanctuary is the only option, it can work if careful consideration is given to equipment needs, setup, and takedown.

In choosing a worship space, consider the following:

1. *How many people will the room comfortably hold?*

Choose a room that fits the proposed number of worshipers. An ideal room is one that allows for an intimate, casual feeling, but also allows room for growth.

A room that is too large may result in these feelings:

- Where are the people?
- This is not a very popular service.
- I don't really know the people in this service.
- I am so far removed from everyone that I can remain anonymous.

It is unlikely that a feeling of warmth and intimacy can be achieved when the congregation is so spread out. Interaction between the worshipers and the worship leaders will probably not take place.

A room that is too small may result in these feelings:

- The chairs are so close together that I feel crowded.
- There are not enough empty seats for my family/friends to sit together.
- It is so crowded that I will never be missed when I am gone.

A room that is crowded is certainly more exciting than a room that is partially filled. Yet, overcrowding can result in a poor sight line for worshipers, causing them to focus only on the backs of heads. Will there be enough space to curve or angle the chairs to allow for elbow room and a good line of sight?

2. How does the room sound?

Rooms do have very distinctive sound qualities. Take time to stand in the room and listen. What do you hear when the room is empty? Are there mechanical sounds, such as air conditioning fans that will be distracting during quiet, meditative times? Can those sounds be removed? Now bring in the people. What does the room sound like when people are entering for worship and fellowship is taking place? What does the room sound like when everyone is singing or speaking together? If the room has a lot of echo or is very dead, will you be able to remedy the problem with a good sound system? (Solving the sound problem will be explained in chapter 2.) And finally, will the sounds of the worship service carry to other rooms in the building? If so, what else will be taking place in the building during worship?

3. Does the room stand alone?

Where are the entrances and exits for the room? Is this a room that serves as a corridor or common passageway to other parts of the building? If it is, you will have to consider ways to close off the room during worship. There is nothing more distracting than doors opening during a worship service. It is helpful to have signs strategically placed around the building that say, "Quiet, please—worship in progress."

Now that you have considered room size, room sound, and room location, you have probably chosen the best possible space for your new service. But what if your chosen space is being used by the most inflexible Sunday school class in the church? How can you accommodate both? This is when sensitive communication skills are needed. Discuss with the Sunday school class the vision and plans for the new worship service. Do not dictate a change, but help them see how they can be a part of this exciting new service. Would they be willing to support this new service by relocating to another room? Help them to understand that this particular room meets the criteria for a new worship space. If a change cannot be made willingly, maybe it is not the right time to begin a contemporary service in your church.

In choosing a worship space, it is important not to take the leftover room that no one wants. Some contemporary services fail due to the unwillingness of the congregation to make necessary changes. A good example is a large urban church that has a beautiful facility, including a well-equipped theater, but was unwilling to ask a class to move from the theater. The contemporary service was begun in a medium-sized, dark basement room. Even though the room was clean (but not odor-free) and decorated with banners, the service failed. What message did the church send to the active congregation and to potential visitors? Apparently, this service is at the bottom of the ladder in importance because the least desirable room in the church was the only room available. Would you feel wanted and welcomed? This church is certainly not giving its best to this worship service. Surely the church members sense it, but if they don't, visitors will tell them by not coming back!

4. What area of the room will be the focal point?

The answer to this question will probably depend on where the words for the songs will be projected. The use of multimedia (projection of song lyrics, movie clips, and creative announcements) is essential to contemporary worship and therefore its projection must be seen easily by all.

In a fellowship hall setting, it is preferable to place the band, singers, worship leaders, and pastors on a raised platform/stage area. The projection screen can be placed above the platform area or to the side.

In a sanctuary setting, try to keep the band, singers, worship leaders, and pastors in front and center as much as possible. This may require moving some chancel furniture. As an option, the band can be placed off to the side with the worship leaders up front and center. A word of caution: The band must be able to see the worship leaders at all times. The placement of the projector and projection screen in the sanctuary may present a problem if the sanctuary design is anything other than contemporary. Some churches have installed a motorized screen in the middle of the chancel area that is beautifully concealed. Others bring in a portable screen each week or install a screen to the side of the chancel area. (Projectors and screens will be discussed in chapter 3.)

The main objective is to create a focal point for people's attention that is uncluttered and easily seen. Occasionally, consider arranging the room in a different configuration. The change will give the congregation a sense of excitement about the service. If the focal point is changed on occasion, the projection screen should be movable or seen easily from its permanent placement.

5. Should there be platforms to raise the level of the worship leaders above the congregation?

Again, this refers to the sight line. You will want to incorporate drama, dance, interviews, and other action components in the service. It is critical for these components to be easily seen. The raised level improves sight problems as well as giving the worship leaders a sense of authority in leading worship. It is an outdated assumption that intimacy is achieved only when the worship leaders are on the same level with the congregation.

What kinds of platforms are needed? Sturdy ones are essential! Other factors to consider are storage, ease of setup, steps, handicap accessibility, and appearance. This may be one of the most expensive items in the budget for this new service. Prices for platforms/staging will range $1,000 and up. Someone in your congregation could design and build staging for you, but it probably won't be lightweight or easy to store. There are many catalogs from which you may order platforms. (See Resource List at the end of this chapter.) If you are using existing staging, you might need to carpet, recarpet, or add skirting to hide the many microphone cords that will be used. Skirting to fit your staging can also be ordered from catalogs. Prices range from $100 to $500.

6. Is additional lighting necessary?

Unless your room has some type of high-powered spotlighting, the answer is definitely, YES! A room with traditional lighting will not set apart the platform area as the focal point. The praise team may not be able to see their words or music, the congregation will not see the faces of the praise team well, and the altar will be in the dark. There is an incredible transformation in all of these things when they are spotlighted. This is certainly a time when you need to bring in a professional. If there are several lighting companies in your area, have each one come to your church to give you a projected design and price. A word of warning: Lighting companies always want to sell you more than you need. Subtract about 10 percent from what they propose and you will be happy. Look at the different types of lights and price ranges in catalogs before you talk with a company. Prices may range from $1,200 to $4,000 for a complete medium-range system.

7. What type of altar will be used?

The focal point of the room should be the altar. Will you place the altar on the platform or on the floor in front of the platform? Will it be round, square, or rectangular? If the room is multipurpose, is the altar portable?

The larger the altar, the more space you have for creating a mood and theme for each service. A beautiful and functional altar could be created by a talented church member. Give the builder the dimensions you require and ask that it complement your room colors and decor. Large casters can be attached to allow for easy moving. A well-crafted altar will be beautiful with or without an altar cloth and will be the focal point of your service.

8. Will there be a place to kneel?

This will present a problem in any room other than a sanctuary or chapel with existing kneelers. It is essential to provide a space for kneeling when a service is designed for the congregation to respond to God's call in their life. Some portable kneelers are comfortable and sturdy but not easy to store. Kneelers can be bought from church supply companies but will not likely fit your room decor. It would be best if the kneelers could be designed to match the altar and staging. This might be another project for a skilled church member.

9. What types of plants and banners will enhance the worship area?

After you have set up your room with the platform area, altar, kneelers, and chairs, step back and look at the whole picture. Where might you fill in with plants and banners? These are the finishing touches that add warmth and beauty to the room. This will also make the statement that you care enough about this service to create the most pleasing worship space possible. This is definitely an area in which your congregation can help. When we purchased two large silk trees for our new service, four large beautiful silk ferns were donated. If you make the specific needs of this service known, you might be pleasantly surprised at the donations you receive. Also, find the people in your church who are gifted in sewing or needlework and meet with them to design banners for the worship space. (See Resource List.)

CHECKLIST #1: THE WORSHIP SPACE
- A room of the proper size
- A room with good sound potential
- An easily accessible room
- A defined worship space with a focal point
- A properly placed projection screen
- A properly placed platform/staging area
- Will there be spotlights?
- Where will the altar be placed?
- Will there be kneelers?
- Will there be plants and banners?

RESOURCE LIST

Platforms and Skirting
Gamble Musical Merchandise
Chicago, IL 60604
Call: 1-800-621-4290
Fax: 1-312-427-7911
Internet: www.gamblemusic.com

Lighting

All Pro Sound Professional Audio and Lighting Catalog
Pensacola, FL 32505
Call: 1-800-9-ALL-PRO
Internet: www.allprosound.com

Altars/Kneelers

Autom
Phoenix, AZ 85040
Call: 1-800-521-2914
Fax: 1-800-582-1166
E-mail: automphx@aol.com

Christian Supply, Inc.
Spartanburg, SC 29301
Call: 1-800-845-7618
Fax: 1-864-595-0800
Internet: www.christiansupply.com
E-mail: chrsupply1@aol.com

The I. Donnelly Co., Inc.
Kansas City, MO 64131
Call: 1-800-821-5372
Fax: 1-816-363-1283
E-mail: idoncoinc@aol.com

Banners

Robert Gaspard Co.
Call: 1-800-784-6868
Fax: 1-800-784-7567
Internet: www.robertgaspardco.com
E-mail: mail@rgaspard.com

PraiseBanners
Call: 1-800-226-6377
Internet: www.praisebanners.com

Majestic Banners
Call or Fax: 1-214-618-0964

Chapter 2
The Sound System

Basic Components

Now begins the really hard "stuff" for those of us who are traditional or new-to-contemporary church musicians—learning about a sound reinforcement system (better known as "all those cords and the big black box with all the tiny knobs on it"). The end result should be evenly distributed sound to all worshipers so there will be no complaints. This is not impossible if you have a good basic knowledge of how a system should work, quality equipment, and a good sound system operator.

Do you really need all this "stuff"? If you plan to use drums, guitars (that will actually be heard), and an electronic keyboard, the answer is YES! All instruments and voices need to be amplified so that there will be a musical blend and a well-balanced sound for all listeners. The sound requirements for a traditional service are different from the contemporary service. You may or may not amplify your traditional choir for sound reinforcement or recording purposes. The majority of miking in the traditional service will be for speaking amplification. But in the contemporary service, the music of the praise band should be properly mixed to achieve the type of sound desired (e.g., soft rock, hard rock, jazz, blues, and bluegrass).

The basic components of a sound system are the microphone, a mixing console, an equalizer, a power amplifier, and loudspeakers. Unfortunately, there are many different types of microphones, mixing consoles, equalizers, amplifiers, and speakers. They vary considerably according to quality and price. So how do you shop for what you need? Where do you start? There are four options to consider:

1. Design the system yourself. This will probably require more time and patience than you would ever want to give to the monumental task. It might be best not to do this if you want to keep your job intact. Assuming you have some professional help from within your congregation, you will still need a good basic knowledge of what is needed and how to install it properly so that you will not make a costly mistake for the church.

2. Go to a musical instrument retail store. Before you go, prepare yourself to feel really stupid when you cannot follow their "sound system-ese" jargon. First, tell them of your need for a quality speech and music sound reinforcement system (that will impress them) and then ask if they have a trained system designer. If they do, ask for a list of installations they have done in the area. They should be very happy to show you their quality work. Then it is your job to talk with someone who uses that system. This will result in finding out more than you wanted to know.

3. Hire a sound contractor or pro audio dealer. Sound contractors or pro audio dealers usually will be equipped to design, sell (their particular brand), and install the system. An important consideration is that reputable contractors and dealers will service and repair systems they have designed and installed. Look for these people in the yellow pages under music or sound systems and equipment. Also ask for recommendations at the local musical instrument store.

4. Hire an independent consultant. This person will design your sound system, purchase it, oversee its proper installation, and then make final adjustments to ensure its proper working order. This person will not be tied to one particular brand of equipment. He or she will want to give you the best possible system and installation for your money in order to maintain an excellent reputation. Remember that you get what you pay for. Hiring a consultant may seem extravagant to your church committee (range of $800 to $8,000), but this person is working for you in all aspects of the job. The best way to find this person is by word of mouth.

When speaking with a professional sound person, you will need to know the following:

- The size of your worship space
- The shape of the room
- The surface coverings on the wall, floor, seats, and so on
- How many people the room will hold
- Details of an existing sound system and whether or not you plan to use it for this worship service
- The planned makeup of the praise team (number and type of instruments and singers)

Learning the Language
Microphones

A microphone is a very simple device that picks up sound vibrations and converts them into electrical energy (the audio signal). This is done by a diaphragm. The diaphragm responds to the sound vibrations around it but does not have a brain to pick and choose what it hears. Therefore, the microphone will always favor the sound that is loudest, even if that is not the sound wanted. So do you need a dynamic, condenser, electret condenser, ribbon, carbon, or piezoelectric microphone? (I warned you that it would be confusing!) These types are named for the way the microphone is designed to transfer the sound to the audio signal. To simplify, you will want to use the dynamic, or electret condenser microphones for a live worship service. They will range in price from $60 to $350 each.

Dynamic microphones are highly dependable and rugged.

Their technology (moving-coil) has been improved enough to reproduce a reasonably true sound.

Electret condenser microphones can be made very small, which make possible some unique close-miking techniques. Electrets require a built-in amplifier that will need to be powered by a battery housed in the microphone case.

There is still more you need to know when choosing a microphone. Do you want a hand-held, stand-mounted, lavalier, contact pickup, pressure response, shotgun, or parabolic design? Once again I will simplify by stating that you will likely use the hand-held (singers), stand-mounted (drums), lavalier (pastor), and contact pickup (acoustic piano or guitar).

The **hand-held microphone** is well insulated to prevent handling noise and for protection from being dropped. This is the most common type of microphone used and can also be mounted on a stand.

Stand-mounted or **boom-mounted microphones** are most commonly used for recording. They may be the electret (small) types and may be useful to you if appearance is of primary importance.

Lavalier microphones are small elements that are designed to clip directly to clothing (also called lapel microphones). They should be used with a wireless transmission system so that the person speaking will have complete freedom to move around.

The **contact pickup microphone** can be purchased as a flexible strip that is affixed to the instrument with sticky wax. It uses the condenser principle and offers exceptional resistance to feedback. The placement of the strip is critical to achieve satisfactory results. You might also want to experiment with miking the instrument along with using the strip. These newer devices will require a little experimentation to achieve the best possible sound.

Microphones are also classified by their pickup pattern. Do

you want an omnidirectional, cardioid, bidirectional, supercardioid, or hemispherical type? Omnidirectionals or cardioids work best for a live worship service.

The omnidirectional elements pick up sound more or less equally from all directions. You may think that this is not what you want because of possible feedback (a "howling" sound—not very worshipful!), but it can be used if sufficient distance is placed between the speakers and the microphone. **Omnidirectional microphones** tend to have much smoother frequency response than directional microphones so they are quite often the best choice.

The **cardioid microphone** is the most popular pickup pattern for worship services. It can help reduce feedback and increase system gain (this is what your sound system operator needs to know).

And finally, microphones are divided into two basic classes: **high-impedance** and **low-impedance**. Most professional microphones are low-impedance devices. This is preferred in live sound reinforcement because when properly connected, they are far less susceptible to additional noise pickup in the cable. What will probably be more important to you is that low-impedance microphones can drive cables hundreds of feet long, whereas high-impedance microphones are limited to cables about twenty feet long.

Believe it or not, there is still one more type of microphone that you need to know about. It has become essential for the contemporary worship service—the **wireless microphone**. These microphones work like a miniature version of a commercial FM broadcasting system. In other words, the sound is transmitted from the microphone or a miniature body pack to a receiver that picks up the frequency signal and is wired to the mixing console. The transmitter and receiver must be tuned to the same frequency. It is possible for more than one wireless microphone to be used at the same time in the same service if each system operates on a different frequency. Check with the microphone company for proper frequency separation. A lavalier microphone for the pastor and at least two hand-held microphones for portable use during the service (taking praises and concerns from the congregation) are suggested. A wireless system will run between $300 and $1,500.

Direct Boxes

This was not listed as a part of the sound system, but should be mentioned at this point. It is advisable to plug electronic instruments (guitars, basses, and keyboard/synthesizers) into a direct box before connecting to the mixer. The direct box is a specially designed signal transformer that takes the high-impedance signal from the instrument and then converts it to a low-impedance signal for the mixing console. A low-impedance signal does not pick up as much extraneous noise. Direct boxes can also prevent the instrument from picking up phantom-power voltages (wireless microphones) and help eliminate the "hum" that is often picked up between equipment. Grounding (or the lack thereof) is very important. It is advisable to buy boxes with a ground lift switch. Direct boxes will cost between $24 and $100.

Mixers and Mixing Consoles

Mixers and mixing consoles are the heart of the sound system. The term *mixer* usually applies to a small unit, having four to twelve input channels that is generally used by live performing groups. These mixers are portable, lightweight, have some built-in effects and graphics, and may contain internal amplifiers to drive external speakers. They are not as quiet or as versatile as their larger brother, the "console." The term *console* applies to a larger unit with more knobs than you will want to count! In other words, it has a lot more versatility.

The job of a mixer and/or console is to combine and reroute

audio signals from a set of signal input channels, to a set of signal output channels, and along the way modify the signal through sound enhancement circuitry. These signals can be modified through the features available on each channel or by sending the signal externally by auxiliary send and return jacks. These enhancement circuitry devices are commonly called sound effects boxes, or in the case of many effects in one box, multisound effects boxes. These devices (signal processors) will be covered later in this chapter.

Each console channel allows total control of the signal routing and the amount, if any, of signal processing. When combined with all other channels, the master blend or "mix" is achieved. The sound operator can send different mixes to different locations. For example, one combination of signals can be sent to the instrumentalist's monitors, another to the singer's monitors, another to the house speakers, and another to the master tape recording, audio/visual, or radio/television output.

All this can be achieved through the use of internal bussing networks. An explanation of this operation can be quite confusing, so think of it as a city transit bus service. Each bus starts at the bus station and has a programmed bus route. If you wish to arrive at a certain destination, you must make the appropriate connections along the way. The same is true inside the mixing console. There can be many bus routes, each one with a different destination. It is a matter of assigning which signals go to which bus route.

The most important advice any good sound person will give you about a mixing console for your service is to always purchase a console with more inputs than you think you will need. Don't try to save money by thinking, "We will never need more inputs than that." The following is a recommended list of very basic inputs:

1. Keyboard
2. Drums
3. Drums
4. Bass Guitar
5. Guitar
6. Guitar or other instrument
7. Synthesizer
8. Lead singer
9. Lead singer
10. Backup singer
11. Backup singer
12. Backup singer
13. Backup singer
14. Pastor
15. Wireless microphone for congregation
16. Wireless microphone for congregation
17. Cassette tape player
18. CD player
19. VCR (sound for video clips)

This does not include microphones for choirs or dramas. You can see that if you are beginning a service with the basics, you should plan to purchase a mixing console with a minimum of 24 channels. The price range for mixers and mixing consoles is $300 to $2,500.

Signal Processors/Sound Effects Boxes

A signal processor (often called sound effects box) refers to a device that changes something about the character of the sound. These devices are not absolutely necessary, but are well worth the additional expense. Three different types of processors will enhance the overall sound:

1. Processors that affect certain portions of the frequency spectrum (low, medium, high). These are the **equalizers** and **filters**.
2. Processors that control the volume of the signal. These are **compressors**, **limiters**, and **noise gates**.
3. Processors that control the perceived spaciousness of the sound. These are for the **reverb** and **delay**.

These processors can be inserted in three different places: between the microphones/instruments and the mixer; between the mixer channels and busses; or between the main mixer outputs and the amplifier. How you want to modify the sound (individually or for the room) will determine their placement. These processors are highly recommended as they will greatly enhance your ability to mix the sound you desire for your congregation. They will range between $180 and $350.

Power Amplifiers

The amplifier will be the last component in your system before the sound comes out of the loudspeakers. Its purpose is to increase the power of the audio signal so that the signal can drive one or more speakers. It is very important to match the power of the amplifier with the capabilities of the speakers. An amplifier with too much power will damage the speakers. They range in price from $180 to $1,100.

Loudspeakers

Loudspeakers change electricity into sound. It would be nice if any speaker would suffice, but as you have already learned from the other sound system components, there are many different types from which to choose. Following are the different classifications of speakers:

Ceiling Loudspeakers. These are speakers mounted in a cluster on the ceiling. Some of the speakers will have a long throw to direct sound to the farthest listeners, some will have a short throw to direct sound over a wide angle to nearby listeners, and some will have the ability to deliver high sound pressure levels. If the ceiling is too low for speakers to be mounted, loudspeakers may be placed at intervals in the ceiling to cover the seating area. *Warning! Speakers recessed in the ceiling are prone to feedback problems!*

Stand or Wall-Mounted Speakers. If your room is not very large, speakers may be mounted on stands or on the wall, in place of the ceiling. Speakers in each corner of the room will give you a stereo effect (two front and two rear speakers). House speakers will range in price from $160 to $800.

Monitors

Stage monitors are placed in close proximity to those who will be listening to them—singers, instrumentalists, actors, pastors, and any other members of the worship team. The volume should be kept as low as possible to minimize feedback paths to open microphones. Monitors are usually wedge-shaped and sit low on the floor, angled up toward the worship team. Monitors will range in price from $100 to $600. There is a new loudspeaker technology that needs to be mentioned here. Speakers are now made with a built-in amplifier. In the old technology, the signal that is sent from the amplifier to the speaker can lose wattage when it must travel a great distance. The new technology will alleviate this problem as the speaker will receive full wattage power from the amplifier.

One final question needs to be answered about your sound reinforcement system: Is mono or stereo better? If speech is the priority in your worship service, stereo doesn't work well. On the other hand, stereo will enhance the sound of your praise team and also can be used to help stop feedback or noise problems. Some churches handle this dilemma by having two subsystems: monophonic for speech and stereo for music. Both can be run from the same console if there are enough output busses.

What I have learned about sound systems has come through experience and an absolute must-have resource: *Guide to Sound Systems for Worship*, edited by Jon F. Eiche (see Resource List).

Are you overwhelmed now? You should be! The most expensive items for a contemporary worship service and the most critical components are the sound system and projection system (see chapter 3). It is extremely important to thoroughly research both systems before you start buying all the gadgets!

CHECKLIST #2: THE SOUND SYSTEM

- Number and types of microphones needed
- Number of direct boxes needed
- Mixing console
- Signal processors
- Power amplifiers
- Number and types of loudspeakers

RESOURCE LIST

Sound Systems

All Pro Sound Professional Audio and Lighting
Pensacola, FL 32505
Call: 1-800-9-ALL-PRO
Internet: www.allprosound.com

Capital Communications Industries (CCI)
Olympia, WA 98507
Call: 1-800-426-8664
Email: 102625.3216@compuserve.com

Worship Resources (Audio-Visual Specialist for the Church)
A complete selection of professional audio-visual and video equipment:
Call: 1-800-486-0305
Fax: 1-800-575-4833
Internet: www.worshipres.com

Books

Jon F. Eiche, ed. *Guide to Sound Systems for Worship.* Milwaukee, Wis.: Hal Leonard Publishing Corp., 1990.
Contact: Hal Leonard Publishing
P.O. Box 13819
Milwaukee, WI 53213

The most essential book for the complete understanding of sound systems and as easy to understand as anyone could make the subject!

Chuck Walthall. *Sound Made Simple.* All Pro Sound. Manual only, CD-ROM version, manual, and CD.

A practical, hands-on guide to setting up and running a sound system. Nontechnical examples will teach you about microphone placement, mixing console controls, and general recommendations about sound system operation. Call: 1-800-9-ALL-PRO.

Chapter 3
The Projection System

Multimedia Presentations

How do we communicate today? Do we communicate the same way we did ten years ago? I know I certainly don't! Ten years ago I would have never imagined checking my e-mail every night and writing letters on a consistent basis. One year ago, I could not imagine e-mailing digital photographs as I do now. I now communicate with the help of multimedia on a daily basis.

If you were trying to start an exciting new business, would you invite a large crowd of people to hear you talk about it? This would be a good place to start, but I think you would do more than just talk. I am sure you would pull out all the stops and whistles. You would probably have a video to show and large, colorful charts for visual explanations. Words alone can communicate, but not nearly as effectively as words in combination with a multimedia presentation. Multimedia can make the people sit up and take notice. Without it, most people will lose interest quickly. We must do all we can to keep people's interest in hearing and seeing God's message for their lives. We must learn to communicate in a visually dynamic way.

How can you present Sunday's message in spoken word, combined with a multimedia presentation? Simple: Put it all on screen. I prefer to do away with the bulletin so that the worshiper is not interacting with a piece of paper in his or her hand. Instead, the worshiper is interacting with his or her eyes forward on a screen that is visually exciting—not static like the bulletin. Let's look at what you will need to make this possible.

There are five different ways to project your service onto a screen: (1) slide projectors; (2) overhead projectors; (3) large-screen televisions; (4) LCD projection panels; and (5) video projectors.

1. Slide Projectors

These are easy to use, provide a bright display, and are relatively inexpensive to maintain. It is ideal to mount the projector on the ceiling so it will be out of the line of sight of the worshiper. Be sure that you can easily get to the carousel on the machine. The remote control can be wired into the projector or it can be a wireless control that is programmable. Some controls have the ability to "fade to black." If your room is fairly dark and the projector can be mounted in close proximity to the screen, you can purchase an inexpensive machine ($200). If you want a much brighter display in a lighter room, the machine will cost considerably more. Some slide projectors have a special lamp that makes them capable of projecting theater-sized pictures. These units may cost as much as a low- to medium-end video projection unit that will be capable of much more. Slides are easy to make on the computer or can be purchased from a Christian music store. The disadvantages are that slides can become jammed and only images that can be made into slides can be used. You will not be able to show video clips or scanned pictures with this projection unit. You would need to use TV/VCR units in your service to accomplish this.

2. Overhead Projectors

These units have a wider range of brightness display (2,000 to 7,000 lumens) than the slide projector, are inexpensive ($250 and up, based on number of lumens), are very portable, and require minimum maintenance. Everything displayed must be put on a transparency. Text can be typed on a computer, then copied onto a transparency with a laser or ink-jet printer of good quality. Transparencies of music lyrics can also be purchased from Christian music stores. The disadvantages are that the image contrast is not as sharp as other types of projectors and the presentation from the overhead projector will be only as good as its operator. Of course this will apply to all machines, but it is much more critical on an overhead, on which the transparencies must be placed and removed manually. The main objection to this is that the operator and machine will be visible to the congregation and likely will distract from worship. There is also the possibility of the "keystone" effect (smaller image at the bottom, which angles to a larger image at the top) caused by tilting the projector up too much. As with the slide projector, you will not be able to show video clips.

3. Large-Screen Televisions

A computer presentation as well as movie clips can be projected through a large-screen television. This may seem like the most affordable option, but first consider that a large-screen television is limited to a group of fifty people or less for good visibility.

4. LCD Projection Panels

This is a lightweight, slim panel that is placed on top of an overhead projector and connected to a computer. Anything that can be generated on the computer can be shown via the overhead projector and in color. The only limitations are the computer's memory and software. There are two types of panels: active-matrix and passive-matrix. The active-matrix type projects a much better quality image but is more expensive. This type ranges in price from $4,500 to $8,000. (For this price, why not just get a video projection unit?) This price does not include the overhead projector. Unfortunately, not just any overhead will do. Manufacturers recommend a minimum output of 3,000 lumens for the projector. Distortion patterns may appear when the projector gets too hot. Make sure that the panel has more than one port (one for computer and one for video). Basic specifications to consider in the LCD panel are screen size, resolution (the higher the pixel number, the better the picture), number of colors, and on-screen feedback for adjusting picture parameters, such as contrast, sharpness, and brightness. Projection panels have many different capabilities and vary widely between brands in price and quality. Therefore, do your comparative homework when considering this option.

5. Video Projectors

The three most widely used projectors are the CRT (Cathode Ray Tube), the LCD (Liquid Crystal Display), and the DLP (Digital Light Processing) types.

CRT (Cathode Ray Tube) Projectors. This type uses three lenses (blue, green, and red) to produce the images. It produces the highest picture resolution and has been around the longest. Prices range from $3,500 to $35,000 on the low end. High brightness CRTs (1,000 to 3,000 ANSI lumens) range from $50,000 to $100,000. (Try getting that past your finance committee!) Few churches use these projectors due to the high cost and the need for permanent installation.

LCD (Liquid Crystal Display) Projectors. This is a single lens projector that is more portable and includes zoom and focus controls. It is less expensive than the CRT types. Prices range from $2,800 to $12,000. Many models come with built-in speakers and more inputs and outputs than LCD panels, so you can connect several simultaneous video sources and switch among them easily. The lower-priced models may limit the size of the projected image to ten feet diagonal. They also may cause some visible pixelization (visible dots) and motion smearing of fast moving images.

DLP (Digital Light Processing) Projectors. This type of projector uses an array of tiny mirrors to reflect and focus light through a lens onto a screen. This is a fairly new technology but one that has proven to be an excellent choice for churches. It is in the $4,000 price range for 600 lumens.

Both the LCD and DLP projectors offer excellent picture resolutions and varied brightness levels. This, along with the fact that they are affordable and easy to use and maintain, makes them the best choice for churches.

Another new technology that large churches (seating over 1,000) might want to consider is the video wall. This process works by dividing a single video output from the computer into a number of projection units stacked on and next to each other behind the screen. This would be best when an unusually large screen is needed. It is obviously more difficult to calibrate multiple units than to adjust a single unit.

Selecting a Projector/Screen

Room Size. Each projector is limited by how far it can project an image. Therefore the placement of the projector in relationship to the screen is critical.

Front-screen vs. Rear-screen Projection. Front-screen projection works well if you can control the ambient light in the room and can place the projector out of the viewer's sight line. Too much light will wash out the images. Rear-screen projection means that the unit is placed in close proximity behind the screen, thus allowing the projected path to be much darker than when the unit is in front. If you have the space needed, hide the projector behind the screen. Also, rear-projection screens are made of darker material and therefore don't reflect unwanted light from the main room.

Audio. Make sure there is an audio output on the projector so the sound can be run through the house system. Treat this signal as you would a keyboard or an electric guitar by using a direct box.

Screen Material. Before choosing the proper screen, you will need to answer several questions. Will you be using transparencies, slides, or computer projection? How many people have to see the image and do they have to read it?

Next, you will need to determine the optimum screen size based on room dimensions, planned service seating size, and room arrangement. There is a generally accepted equation to find the recommended screen height for your worship space: *the distance in feet from the screen to the farthest viewer divided by 8 should equal the height of the screen.*

You will also need to decide whether you want the screen to be portable, wall- or ceiling-mounted, and whether it needs to be manual or electric (if it is retractable). If it can be permanently mounted, I recommend a flat, wall-mounted screen, which will provide a bright, uniform image with no color shift regardless of the angle from which you view the image. However, if you must move the screen, there are quality portable screens available that are very easy to assemble.

Screens will range in price from $100 for an AV format (square) tripod to $1,000 or higher for a video format (rectangle) electric screen. For a very large room that requires a high-quality screen you will spend several thousand dollars. If you plan to purchase a medium-range video projection unit, plan to purchase at least a medium-range ($500) screen to get your money's worth from the projection unit. Splurge if you can.

Before making a decision on projection units and screens, have the choices you are considering demonstrated in your worship space. Even better, have two or three different units compared at the same time in your worship space. Yes, this is common practice with companies that provide this equipment. If a particular company doesn't agree to a side-by-side comparison, don't consider that brand!

Computer Generated Presentations

This is computer lingo for a slide presentation created on a computer. A word of encouragement: If I can learn how to do this in one easy lesson taught by a high school student, anyone can learn! Well, maybe it was a little more than one easy lesson, but the point is that within a few months I became quite the expert. I am not going to explain in detail what to type on your computer to create the slides because every software program is different. But I will give you some pointers and then you must study your own software manual to learn how to set up the best format that suits your needs.

Most churches with whom I have spoken use Microsoft Office PowerPoint software. There are other programs that are comparable, such as Alpha BRAVO and Corel Show. These programs usually retail for $300 to $400. Whichever program you use, your goal will be to create the most readable presentation for the worshipers. There is nothing worse than being expected to participate in a service but not being able to read the words on the screen; or worse, not being able to make out a clear image of any kind (imaginations can run wild and the mood has been lost).

Start by learning to type your text-only slides. These slides will be for the words to songs and congregational responses, such as a call to worship, unison prayer, communion liturgy, affirmation of faith, and so on. The text will be more readable on a blank background (no pictures other than borders) and a traditional, easy-to-read font. Most people use a bright blue background with a bright yellow font (Arial or Times New Roman) that is bold and shadowed in black. These colors give the sharpest contrast, making the text the most readable. Black to white is not a good choice unless the room is extremely dark. The size of the font should be 32-point or larger so that it will be readable from any distance. After projecting a few slides on your screen, you will learn what margins should be used. Whichever font and color scheme you use, be consistent throughout the presentation. It is difficult for a reader when each slide changes drastically.

Here is an interesting fact my right-hand computer person taught me. Times New Roman is called a "serif" font. Serifs are the little points and decorations at the ends and corners of the letters. Arial is a "sans-serif" font, because it has no ornaments. Serifs aren't just for looks, they lead the eye and make things easier to read. No newspaper is printed in all sans-serif fonts, because of the small typeface. Serif fonts are easier to read in small typefaces. The basic rule of thumb is that sans-serif fonts should be used for large text and serif fonts for small text.

When typing a responsive reading, type the leader's words in white and the congregation's words in yellow. The contemporary congregation will relate this to the traditional bulletin, in which responses are set in bold print. I like to type the title of a song slide in white and the words in yellow. Then I type the copyright information and CCLI number (see next chapter) at the bottom of the slide in a smaller font (24-point) in white and italics.

The opening slides of your presentation can be one of the best places to get all the announcements out of the way before the service begins. We usually have six to eight announcement slides that run for five minutes prior to the service and through the initial welcome and opening time of the service. These slides can be changed manually by the computer operator or can be set to run on a timer, changing at timed intervals. This is a time to be as creative as possible with your slide design. Learn the numerous options that are available to you with your software and other resources. Import pictures from the hard drive of your computer or from other sources (CD-ROM programs or the Internet); use the pictures as background to the text; animate pictures or text; or videotape someone giving the announcements in an interesting setting and in short segments. Always check your presentation on screen prior to the service. What looked spectacular on your computer monitor might be a major disappointment when projected on a large screen. High contrast of colors is vitally important! All of these ideas will add interest to your announcements and catch the congregation's attention.

With the announcements out of the way, the main body of the presentation can begin with a specific theme. For example, if the service is about baptism, use a lot of water pictures as fillers between songs. Plan to have a slide on screen at all times. Think of the presentation as the bulletin. You will need to let the congregation know what is coming next, e.g., prayer time, offering, special music, scripture reading. Some wonderful ways to use the advancing technology are to scan in a baby's picture to put on screen while he or she is being baptized or to put new members' pictures on screen while introducing them. You can put these pictures directly into the computer if you use a digital camera.

People from your congregation need to be recruited to create the presentation and to run it. Find someone with a fair amount of computer knowledge, if possible, and someone able to give approximately two hours a week to create the presentation. It is possible to train someone with a desire to learn this process. There are many computer software classes available now to train those who don't want to learn by trial and error. This visual presentation of your service is just as critical as the sound!

Adding movie clips or your own videos to the presentation is challenging and fun. There is nothing that will capture the attention of the worshiper more than a true-to-life example. When a VCR is plugged into your video projection unit, you can switch from the computer generated presentation to video by pressing the button on your projection unit's remote control. Hint: Plug a separate monitor into your VCR to cue the movie clip or video to its exact position for a smoother transition. As this process is practiced, the transition from computer to video will become smoother. Check all adjustments prior to the service such as the high/low contrast. If the video is too dark, you can make the adjustment on the remote control. Be creative and have fun, and remember that this does not take the place of the spoken Word, but enhances, complements, and augments the Word.

Buying a Computer

(I am indebted to Marcus Ledbetter, my invaluable right-hand man for contemporary worship at Munsey, for his contribution to this section on computers.)

It's time to buy a computer. What kind do you need? What brand is the best? How many gigs and megs and other confusing units of measure do you need to have? These are the questions that stump most people when they go to buy their first computer. If you are blessed enough to have a good, nonbiased source in your church to answer these questions, by all means, take advantage of this person's expertise. Of course, you should know enough to avoid unnecessary purchases. No matter how much of an "expert" a person may be, you are the one who knows what the computer needs to do. In other words, just because one of the high school kids is a computer-whiz, you will not need that "Extreme 3D" game accelerator card for running PowerPoint presentations!

One of the first questions to answer is what type of computer to buy. You really only have two choices: PC or Macintosh. There are advantages to both, and both are excellent machines. The first question you should examine is, "What is the rest of the church using?" If your church is a Macintosh-based church, don't be the one standout that uses a PC. You'll be sorry when you have a hard time sharing files with the other users. Don't rock the boat by buying noncompatible equipment. The fundamental differences between Macintosh and PC are mostly technical differences that people in video production and other highly technical computer work care about. Either machine will work for you.

Those funny words computer salespeople throw around all

the time—gigs, megs, Kbps, MHz—are all units of measure for computers. These terms describe either speed or storage capacity. A megabyte (meg) is the most common term in computer lingo. Hard drives and memory are most commonly referred to in terms of megs. Recently, hard drives have become so large, they are referred to in gigabytes (gigs) rather than megs. A gigabyte is simply 1,000 megabytes. Any new computer will probably come with no less than 3 to 4 gigabytes of hard drive space, and no less than 32 megs of RAM (memory). In fact, I would upgrade the RAM to 64 or more, preferably 128 megs, to run a computer generated presentation with lots of photos. Your hard drive space needs to be large enough to hold all of the applications you use. This is strictly a quantity issue. The more hard drive space you have, the less you'll have to store on Zip® disks, floppies, and CDs.

To fully appreciate the need for large amounts of RAM, it helps to understand the purpose of memory. Memory is basically scratch paper for your computer. In grade school, you were often allowed scratch paper during math tests to work out the problems. It would have taken a lot longer to work a large problem if you had to do it all in your head. But, when you had sheets of paper to write out the problem and work it through step by step, it went a lot faster. The reason it was faster is that you had all the data as you went along to refer back to during the process of solving the problem. The same is true with computers. The computer stores data in RAM so it can get to it faster without having to "recompute" data. The more RAM your computer has, the more efficient it is and the faster it will get the work done. This is especially true when you have multiple programs open at once. They are all competing for that memory, and if there isn't enough to go around, you'll have to wait.

A good rule of thumb in computer buying is to avoid the "top-of-the-line." If you buy the newest chip on the market, you're paying extra because it's the most powerful to date. *Within six months the prices drop considerably because computer technology develops so quickly.* Buy one to two notches below the top of the line for value. Purchase 64 to 128 megs of RAM, 4 to 5 gigs of hard drive space, and a good graphics card (4 to 8 megs of RAM). This will ensure accurate image display through your projector. Make sure you have a CD-ROM drive, and if possible, a DVD drive. A DVD drive will read the CD-ROM disks, but will also play the new DVD disks, which will be the emerging standard. A Zip® drive is an invaluable tool. A Zip® disk will store about seventy times the amount of data that can be stored on a floppy. You can use Zip® disks to store all the songs and images that make building a presentation easier, and they are great for storing old presentations, too.

Purchase a 17-inch monitor if possible. Since it is larger, it will be easier on your eyes, but remember that with higher resolutions, you still need to make the text large enough to be viewed on the big screen. If your church can go one step further into visual media and purchase cameras for video production (e.g., taping announcements, interviews, on-site mission work, and so on), a very helpful resource is *Media Ministry Guidebook* by Len Wilson and Connie Pack (see Resource List).

CHECKLIST #3: THE PROJECTION SYSTEM
- What type of projection unit will be used?
- What type and size of screen will be used?
- What will be projected?
- Will videos be used?
- Will you need a computer?
- Have people been recruited to create and run the presentation?

RESOURCE LIST

Projection Systems
All Pro Sound Professional Audio and Lighting
Pensacola, FL 32505
Call: 1-800-9-ALL-PRO
Internet: www.allprosound.com

Capital Communications Industries (CCI)
Olympia, WA 98507
Call: 1-800-426-8664
Email: 102625.3216@compuserve.com

Communication Resources
Canton, OH
Call: 1-800-992-2144
Fax: 1-330-493-3158
E-mail: order@ComResources.com
Internet: www.ChurchArtOnline.com

Fowler Productions, Inc.
Norman, OK 73070
Call: 1-800-729-0163
Fax: 1-800-445-2845
Internet: www.fowlerinc.com
Specializes in projection systems for churches.

J & J Graphics and Designs (slides)
39000 John Dr.
Canton, MI 48187
Call: 1-313-453-0697
Fax: 1-313-453-0698

Modern Sound Pictures, Inc. (audio-visual/video equipment)
Omaha, NE 68102

Call: 1-800-228-9584
Fax: 1-402-341-8487
Internet: www.modernsoundpictures.com

Phil Barfoot Music Co. (slides and overheads)
P.O. Box 4629
Chatsworth, CA 91313

Shepherd Ministries (projection systems)
2221 Walnut Hill Lane
Irving, TX 75038-4410
Call: 1-214-580-8000
Fax: 1-214-580-1329

Books and Software
Len Wilson. *The Wired Church: Making Media Ministry CD-ROM.* Nashville: Abingdon Press, 1999.
A how-to book plus CD-ROM for those who implement multimedia digital technology in worship services and in Christian education curricula. Shows how to design media ministry, describes the tools and costs, and provides a guide for building a championship team. (Requirements: Windows 95 or higher, 486 PC or higher, 16MB RAM, 12MB free hard disk space, CD-ROM drive.) Available through Cokesbury.

Len Wilson and Connie Pack. *Media Ministry Guidebook.* Published by Ginghamsburg United Methodist Church, 6759 South County Rd. 25-A, Tipp City, Ohio. Call: 1-937-667-1069; Fax: 1-937-667-5677.

Monty L. Winters, ed. *How to Find, Select and Buy the Right Video Projection System for Your Church or Ministry.* Fowler Productions, Inc. 1-800-729-0163.

Chapter 4
Necessary Licenses

Make It Legal

The making of unauthorized copies of all copyrighted material is strictly illegal. The key word here is *illegal*. We do not expect churches to do anything illegal, yet many churches that preach the gospel are guilty of stealing intellectual property by illegal copying of music. The United States Copyright Law (effective January 1, 1976) grants to any copyright owner the exclusive rights to original material for a term that is equal to the length of the life of the author/creator plus seventy-five years. Only the copyright administrator has the privilege of reproducing the work. If any other party wants to reproduce the material in some manner, permission must be obtained from the copyright administrator.

Thank heavens for licensing agencies that were formed to help church musicians do their jobs within the confines of the law and with ease. These agencies keep us from having to call numerous publishing companies and studio representatives every week and pay weekly fees for the many copyrighted materials used in worship. They have kept our jobs from becoming an administrative nightmare! If these agencies did not exist, I would have to compose music, write liturgies, and make my own videos for each worship service. Instead, I pay an annual fee to Christian Copyright Licensing, Inc. (CCLI) and the Motion Picture Licensing Corporation (MPLC) so my weekly tasks will be much simpler. From time to time I must call for permission to use other copyrighted materials that are not covered under these two licenses, but I do so gratefully since most materials I choose to use are already covered.

The largest licensing agency is Christian Copyright Licensing, Inc. (see Resource List). The license covers more than 100,000 songs from more than 2,000 publishers and songwriters. After paying an annual fee, your church will receive a license with your "SongSelect Activation Code" printed on it. This is the number that you must display on all copies you make. You will also receive a current License Manual that will be your resource for all the songs that can be used. The cost to your church is based on your church's average weekly worship attendance for all services.

Your active license grants you permission to:

- Print song and hymn texts in bulletins, programs, liturgies, and songsheets.
- Create overhead transparencies, slides, or use any other format whereby song texts are visually projected, such as computer graphics and projection.
- Arrange, print, and copy your own vocal or instrumental arrangements of songs, where no published version is available.
- Record your worship services by audio or video means, provided you only record "live" music (instrumental and vocal). Accompaniment tracks cannot be reproduced. Information concerning fees you may charge and other information is available from the company.

Your active license does *not* grant you permission to:

- Photocopy or duplicate octavos, cantatas, musicals, handbell music, keyboard arrangements, vocal scores, orchestrations, or other instrumental works.
- Translate songs from English into another language. This can only be done with the approval of the respective copyright administrator.
- Rent, sell, lend, or distribute copies made under the Church Copyright License to individuals or groups outside the church, or to other churches.

- Assign or transfer the Church Copyright License to any other church or group without CCLI's approval.

This is an annual license. All terms are in effect only when the license is active. If the license is not renewed, all rights are terminated effective on the expiration date.

Additional helpful products can be ordered through CCLI to help you in copyright issues, reporting, and finding the songs you want to use.

Another agency that covers contemporary Christian music is LicenSing. See Resource List for complete information.

The U.S. Copyright Act also states that all home videocassettes shown outside one's personal residence are "public performances," and mandates that they be licensed. Noncompliance with the law is subject to statutory damages starting at $500 per exhibition. This legal requirement applies equally to profit and nonprofit facilities, whether or not an admission is charged. MPLC, the authorized licensing agent for Hollywood studios and producers ranging from Disney to Warner Brothers, provides the necessary public performance license so you can comply with the Federal Copyright Law. The Motion Picture Licensing Corporation offers a renewable, annual license for $95 per congregation. Additional programs (e.g., a church preschool) may be on the same license at a minimal additional fee. Public performances may take place only at the location you specify on your license. The license doesn't cover advertising specific titles to the general public or charging a fee to view them. The agency is working to include more Christian producers, such as Word, but for now, you have to obtain permission through the individual producer or distributor. Also, if you want to show an MGM movie, you have to get permission through MGM, since they do not have an agreement with MPLC.

If your church service is televised, none of the licensing options discussed here will cover broadcast rights to the videos used as part of the service. Contact the studio directly and be ready to pay more.

If you want to videotape a television show (not a movie) or ad, contact your local television affiliate. You will probably be told that what is broadcast on public airways is public domain, but it is always better to ask. It will be good to develop a relationship with the people who work at the television stations, because they can assist you with your media presentations in many ways. In my experience they are always very helpful.

Where do you find a movie clip for your service? You might find a person in your congregation who is a real "movie buff," but if not, try these interesting resources. The Internet Movie Database and Harbinger Communications, Inc. will help you begin your research (see Resource List).

CHECKLIST #4: NECESSARY LICENSES
- CCLI License
- MPLC License

RESOURCE LIST

Christian Copyright Licensing, Inc.
17201 N.E. Sacramento
Portland, OR 97230
Call: 1-800-234-2446
E-mail: support@ccli.com
Internet: www.ccli.com

Criterion Pictures USA, Inc.
8238-40 Lehigh
Morton Grove, IL 60053
Call: 1-800-890-9494
Fax: 1-847-470-8194
Criterion is a new, independent, nontheatrical film licensor that has managed to fill in the gaps the others have left.

Harbinger Communications, Inc.
Call: 1-800-320-7206
Fax: 1-847-622-0830
Harbinger has a library of original video and multiprojector slide presentations designed for use in the church. These resources are available to rent for $35 to $45 and are relatively short, self-contained, and can be used in a wide variety of applications. Call for a catalog and demo video.

The Internet Movie Database
Internet: http://us.imdb.com
This free database aims to capture any and all information associated with movies from across the world, from the earliest cinema to the very latest releases. Thousands of films are catalogued here, making it an amazingly comprehensive reference. It has a powerful search tool that allows you to key in plot summaries, character names, movie ratings, titles, key words or quotes, and much more. It is the closest thing to a "motion picture concordance" available.

LicenSing
Logos Productions, Inc.
6160 Carmen Ave. East
Inver Grove Heights, MN 55076-4422
Call: 1-651-451-9945
Fax: 1-800-328-0200

Motion Picture Association of America
15503 Ventura Blvd
Encino, CA 91436
Call: 1-818-995-6600
Any specific questions you have about legal use of motion pictures can be answered here.

The Motion Picture Licensing Corporation
5455 Centinela Ave.
P.O. Box 66970
Los Angeles, CA 90066-6970
Call: 1-800-462-8855
Fax: 1-310-822-4440

Swank Motion Pictures, Inc.
201 S. Jefferson Ave.
St. Louis, MO 63103-2579
Call: 1-800-876-5577
Fax: 1-314-289-2192
Internet: www.swank.com
Swank will cover nearly every secular title MPLC misses.
Swank is the nation's largest source of motion pictures available to the nontheatrical market.

Chapter 5
The Worship/Praise Team

The Director of Worship
Now that your worship space is designed, you have decided on a complete sound and projection system, and you have the necessary licenses, who will lead the service?

First, hire a director of contemporary worship. This is the person who will be responsible for all the details of the service. The pastor cannot be expected to recruit and train musicians, run sound, create the visual presentation, put it all together on the day of the service, and still be prepared to preach. In small- to medium-sized churches that have a part-time musician on staff, consider increasing that position to full-time if the musician fits the criteria. In medium- to large-sized churches that have a full-time musician already running a full program, it will be necessary to hire another person to take on the responsibilities of contemporary worship. It will take a minimum of sixteen hours per week to produce this service after it is up and running.

In choosing a person to oversee the development of this service, consider the following:
- A person who has a true heart for ministry—one who desires to bring people together to worship God
- A person who agrees and resonates with the vision and mission of the church and the vision for this contemporary service
- A person with a strong music background
- A person with a theological/worship background—someone who understands the components of worship
- A person with strong organizational and leadership skills

The job description for this person may include any or all of the following:

1. Educate the congregation about the purpose and goals of the service.
2. Articulate the needs of this service to the staff and congregation.
3. Be a pastor to all those involved.
4. Set musical standards and requirements for the praise team.
5. Recruit and train singers, instrumentalists, and sound operators.
6. Act as main leader for the team in the overall design of the service.
7. Choose music to be used each week.
8. Prepare scripts and worship notebooks for the praise team.
9. Oversee the setup for worship (room, platform area, sound system, altar, chairs).
10. Lead praise team rehearsals.
11. Work with the other components of worship (drama, dance).
12. Create the bulletin and/or visual presentation.
13. Oversee advertising for the service.
14. Set a budget with the finance committee and approve all expenditures for the service.

The director should consider recruiting and training laypeople to do some of the above jobs. Have these laypeople create the PowerPoint presentation every week, design the altars, oversee the room setup, and lead sectional rehearsals. The first five items will be discussed in more detail as follows. Additional responsibilities of the director of worship will be covered in part 2, "Implementing the Service."

1. Educating the Congregation

This cannot be emphasized enough. I truly believe that the success of a new service will be due in part to the education that is given to the congregation. The purpose of the service should be explained by the pastor from the pulpit. The new contemporary worship director can speak in each adult Sunday school class and offer a time for questions and answers. Updates on your progress can be printed in your church newsletter, and professional posters can be printed to publicize your goals for the service. All of this will convey the message that this service is being well thought out and planned and that it is being given a place of priority in the life of the church.

2. Articulating the Needs of the Service to the Staff and Congregation

Make a list of every minute detail you can think of that will be needed to begin this service. You will be overwhelmed by it all. And that is exactly the point. No one person (i.e., the director) can do it alone. Publish your list (with a brief explanation of what is required by each task) for the staff and congregation. Pray, and expect God to send you the help that is needed.

3. Being a Pastor

The director of worship is not only a detail person for the service, but should also become a pastor to all those involved. This will include all persons involved in the service: setup/takedown crew; sound and visual crew; ushers/greeters; publicity team; altar design team; and anyone else who gives their time and talents to this service. All of these persons need to be encouraged in the faith and held accountable to their commitment that they might become better disciples for our God.

In order to be a pastor to all these people, it would be advisable to train a layperson to be the worship coordinator. This person can take on the responsibility of the many details that need to be handled one hour prior to and during the service. It will be his or her job to see that everything is in place and running smoothly. This job is equal to that of a stage manager in a theatrical performance. This person should enable your worship service to flow more smoothly.

4. Setting Musical Standards and Requirements for the Praise Team

Begin by listening to many different kinds of contemporary Christian music. Look at the list of the current top twenty-five praise and worship songs (available through CCLI). These songs are comparable to the top twenty-five hymns that cross all denominational lines. Listen to several different recordings of these songs to choose a style you like and one you think you will be able to achieve with your musicians. Describe the style you are trying to achieve both verbally and on paper so you can clearly communicate with your musicians what is acceptable and what is not. I began with several bluegrass guitarists, although this was definitely not the style I wanted. I played for them examples of what I did want and explained the difference in the two styles. For most of them, this meant that they would have to take a crash course in chords they were not use to playing, like B-flat! I knew this would be a real stretch for them, but they were willing to give it a try. A sense of accomplishment won them over quickly.

When you know what sound you are trying to create, decide which songs you will use. If you truly want your congregation to be a singing congregation, you must choose singable songs. Learn the difference between music that is meant for performance and music that is singable by the average worshiper. (Music resources are listed in the Resource List.) Evaluate the following in every song:

Is it a singable range? For the nontrained, out-of-shape singer, the range is only one octave, from the B below middle C (men sing an octave lower). This may be a little uncomfortable for the trained singer as well as somewhat boring, but keep in mind that the service should be designed to involve all worshipers.

Is the melody line singable? Some melodies seem to move along well and suddenly hit a bump in the road. Why? It is probably because of the use of an awkward interval. Rule out those songs, as that bump in the road will never seem to smooth out.

Is the rhythm interesting? The rhythm truly sets the style and mood of the song. Does it depict the text well? Will the non-trained musician be able to easily feel/catch it? Complicated rhythm patterns should be reserved for praise team specials.

Does the text reflect your church's beliefs? Look carefully at the text. Does it say what your church believes? There are several songs in our worship book that we will not use because the emphasis is placed on something we do not teach. Remember that there are as many different beliefs and perspectives in these songs as there are composers. They won't all be suitable for your church. It is very important to try to use a good mix of praise choruses with repeated phrases as well as songs with meatier text.

Is the language inclusive? You will have to search for texts that are inclusive, but more are being written every year. Another option is to contact the composer and ask for permission to make textual changes for your congregation. You do not, under any circumstance, have the right to change any words in a copyrighted song. You might be pleasantly surprised, though, at how willing some composers are for you to make minor changes in the text in order to use their song in your service. You can obtain the information you need to contact the composer from CCLI.

With these criteria in mind, choose a list of songs (six to eight) with which to begin your service. These will not need to be theme-oriented, but rather the "traditional" contemporary songs of praise and worship. Choose two that can be used as upbeat, opening songs, two that are more reflective and worshipful, and two that are prayerful.

Your musical standards have been set by the style you have chosen. The requirements for the praise team are simply to be in one accord to work to achieve what you have set before them.

5. Recruiting and Training Singers, Instrumentalists, and Sound Operators

If you have been to any contemporary worship workshops or have read other articles and resources, you may be under the impression that you will need to recruit professional singers and instrumentalists. This is not feasible, or necessary, for most small- to medium-sized churches. It will be to your benefit to recruit only from your current church membership. This will build a sense of ownership in the service. If you cannot recruit a person for a position that you feel is vital, then recruit from outside the church.

Survey your congregation for people willing to be a part of the praise team as singers or instrumentalists. Review that survey and contact each one personally with an invitation to be at the first rehearsal. The first few rehearsals will become a tryout for both you and the participant to see if his or her skills will match the expectations.

First, decide on the name that you will give to each team of people in the service so you will be consistent from the beginning. I have heard many different names but settled on these: the two singers in front are the Worship Leaders; the backup singers are the Praise Team Singers; and the instrumentalists are the Praise Team Band. These people, along with the pastor, sound and video operator, and dancers or actors used in the service are called the Worship Team.

How many people should be on a praise team? That will be determined by the results of your survey. You will choose either to work with what you have or to go out and recruit more. You can have as few as one worship/song leader and a keyboard player or as many singers as your platforms and sound system will accommodate, along with a backup choir and full band or orchestra. Somewhere in between these two options would be a good place to start. I hope you can begin with more than one worship/song leader. One is a lonely number on the platform when trying to generate excitement for worship.

Begin with a larger group of singers and instrumentalists than you will use each week in service. We began with eighteen singers and ten instrumentalists. Weekly we use four to six singers and four to six instrumentalists. The singers consist of: two worship leaders (male/female, both singing melody to help the congregation to hear the melody in both the male and female range), one soprano (not necessary if the female worship leader is a strong soprano), one alto, one tenor, and one bass. Each singer has his or her own microphone. The instrumentalists consist of one main keyboard (electronic), one synthesizer for additional sounds, one drummer, one electric bass, one electric guitar, and one acoustic guitar. At first, we also had a flute player. This was very beneficial to the congregation for hearing the melody of a new song. We now have a very talented saxophone player. Don't be scared to include other instruments. They will not play all the time, but will add a beautiful variety when used occasionally.

We have tried several different rotation systems. In one system, a monthly schedule that shows the singers and instrumentalists to be used each Sunday is mailed to each person. If someone has a conflict, he or she can call the director to make changes. This requires a lot of calling! Another system assigns everyone to an A or B team. The teams are assigned to specific Sundays for six months and a team leader is designated for each month. The team leader contacts the team weekly to decide which persons can lead, which persons can sing backup (there should be more than one alto on each team), and which persons will be the instrumentalists. The instrumentalists can always work out their Sundays between themselves.

You might choose to use all your singers for the first six months (several on one microphone) to teach new songs. There is safety in numbers! This would also give your singers confidence in going solo on each part. Always have all parts sing unison when teaching a new song. After the congregation is confident of the melody, add the alto, tenor, and bass parts.

At the first rehearsal, discuss the purpose of the praise team, set goals for the first six months, and hand out written expectations. Include in the expectations rehearsal dates and times, how much music is to be learned, if the music is to be memorized or not, if the ability to learn an SATB part on their own is necessary, and so on. Tell the team that it will take time and hard work to develop the desired sound. It will not happen overnight or even within the first six weeks. Also, it is important to understand that you will not want the sound to remain the same. It should always be evolving.

I suggest rehearsing for a minimum of six weeks before beginning your new service. During this time, the people involved will get a feel for whether or not this is a ministry in which they want to take part. This can serve as your audition time. Or, you may prefer to choose the new team members by auditioning first. Teach them a simple praise chorus and have them perform for you or a group of evaluators. Whatever method you use, be specific and consistent with each person!

When you have your praise team up and running, the director's job becomes one of building and maintaining a healthy team. It is important to understand what makes a healthy praise team.

1. A healthy team understands and is committed to the

team's purpose. *A shared vision and goals will require teamwork.* The director will need to model the team's vision for them at all times.

2. Orient new members to the vision and purpose of the praise team. Don't assume they will already know these things or will pick them up by osmosis.

3. Spend time developing leaders for both the singers and the instrumentalists. This will be vital to the growth of the program and will certainly help when the director needs to be away from the church.

4. Create times for community building. Plan gatherings where people can come together and see that they are indeed a team. If you use rotating teams, plan to meet together with the full team every four to eight weeks. Use this time to teach new music, reinforce the purpose and goals, evaluate your progress, and most important, affirm the ministry.

5. An effective director will care for each team member. Focus on the people individually by sending special notes for birthdays, anniversaries, or a thank-you for their contributions. Always give team members an opportunity to share their concerns. Listen and respond so they will know that they have been heard.

(The praise team will be discussed further in chapter 8.)

The Sound System Operator

How important is the sound operator? This person can make or break the worship service. A poorly trained or non-trained sound operator can destroy the worshipful mood set by beautiful music and dynamic preaching. The sound operator is a vital part of the worship team and should be trained and supported. When recruiting a person for this vital role, look for someone who is committed to the many extra hours required for the setup, rehearsal, service time, takedown, and general maintenance of the system.

Get to know the microphones, mixing console, and the monitoring system as well as you know your car. A good resource book, system installer, or sound consultant can explain proper microphone technique, how all the knobs on the mixing console work together, and how to send a different mix of sound to each of the speakers.

The monitor speakers for the singers and instrumentalists are quite often the most difficult aspect of the sound operator's job. The operator needs to spend time listening to the monitors during rehearsals. This will enable the operator to better understand the musicians' needs.

The operator's most important tool for the job is his or her ears. Listening critically will help the operator to create the most natural sound possible in the room. Being "tuned in" at all times during the service is critical to the job.

A Troubleshooting Plan

When things go wrong, and they will, remember these two words first: Stay calm! Then follow the plan you have devised for checking all components. Don't wait until a problem arises in the service to decide that you really need a troubleshooting plan. Write or type your plan and post it in an obvious spot. Here are a few hints:

- Check to ensure that every component is plugged in and turned on.
- Check battery-operated equipment to ensure that the batteries are fresh and properly installed.
- Carefully examine all equipment settings (especially the mute button).
- Check to ensure that the signal path is complete.

There will be many other ways you will need to check your specific system. It will be much easier to check your system if you have labeled all inputs, outputs, and plugs during installation. Most important, keep your design and installment plans handy. They should answer most of your questions. If your sound operator was not a part of the purchase and installation of the system, bring in someone to explain in detail each piece of equipment for your particular system. Practice and experience are truly the best teachers. Just make sure that the operator's practice takes place before the first service!

CHECKLIST #5: THE WORSHIP/PRAISE TEAM
- Hire a director of worship.
- Design a job description for the director.
- Decide on ways to educate the congregation.
- Make a list of needs for the service.
- Choose a style of music.
- Choose a list of songs to teach first.
- Recruit singers and instrumentalists.
- Set up a system for scheduling the praise team.
- Create specific goals for the praise team.
- Plan the first rehearsal.
- Consider using a worship coordinator for the service.
- Make sure the sound operator is ready.
- Label all inputs, outputs, and plugs.
- Make copies of your troubleshooting plan.

RESOURCE LIST

Workshops
International Worship Institute
Call: 1-800-627-0923
Internet: www.worshipinstitute.com
More than 120 workshops taught by over 40 dynamic speakers.

Worship Leader Workshop
Call: 1-800-245-SONG
Internet: www.maranathamusic.com
Idea-packed workshops for pastors, worship leaders, choral directors, singers, musicians, and sound technicians.

Publishers/Suppliers
Vineyard Music Group
P.O. Box 68025
Anaheim, CA 92817-8025
Call: 1-800-852-VINE

Wellsprings Unlimited, Inc.
204 Sevens Court
Burnsville, MN 55306
Call: 1-612-890-3863

Songbooks
Cokesbury Chorus Book: Praise and Worship Music for Today's Church. Expanded Edition. Nashville: Abingdon Press, 1999. Call: 1-800-672-1789.

Come Celebrate! Jesus! Music for Contemporary Worship, Songbook 1. Cathy Townley and Mike Graham, eds. Nashville: Abingdon Press, 1997. Call: 1-800-672-1789.

Come Celebrate! Praise and Worship! Music for Contemporary Worship, Songbook 1. Cathy Townley and Mike Graham, eds. Nashville: Abingdon Press, 1997. Call: 1-800-672-1789.

Come Celebrate! Music for Contemporary Worship, Songbook 1. Cathy Townley and Mike Graham, eds. Nashville: Abingdon Press, 1995. Call: 1-800-672-1789.

Come and Worship
Integrity Music, Inc.
Mobile, AL 36685
Call: 1-334-633-9000

Praise Hymns and Choruses
Maranatha! Music
P.O. Box 31050
Laguna Hills, CA 92654-1050
Call: 1-800-444-4012
Fax: 1-800-245-7664

Praise and Worship Songbooks
Integrity Music, Inc.
Mobile, AL 36685
Call: 1-334-633-9000

Songs for Praise and Worship
Word Music
P.O. Box 141000
Nashville, TN 37202
Call: 1-888-324-9673

How-to Books
Contemporary Praise & Worship Guitar by Paul Baloche
Skillful Resources
P.O. Box 2101
Lindale, TX 75771

Drums in Worship by Mike Kinard
LeMar Boschman Ministries
P.O. Box 130
Bedford, TX 76095

Music

Hosanna! Music Recording and Songsheets Program
Hosanna! Music
Integrity Direct, Inc.
P.O. Box 5205
Clifton, NJ 07015-9785

Every eight weeks you receive a tape or CD and accompanying songsheets from their *Praise and Worship* series. Songsheets include separate guitar chord charts and overhead masters for transparencies for every song. You can return any set you don't want within fifteen days.

Interlinc
P.O. Box 680848
Franklin, TN 37068
Call: 1-615-790-9080

The most current music videos, CDs, and tapes by contemporary Christian artists.

MasterSong Arrangement
Call: 1-800-245-SONG
Internet: www.maranathamusic.com

A single arrangement includes rhythm charts, keyboard and synthesizer arrangement, piano accompaniment, three-part vocal arrangement, and overhead transparency master.

Music Mansion MIDI Store
Call: 1-800-880-MIDI
Internet: www.musicmansion.com

The largest supplier of MIDI products in the USA.

Raise Praise Music
Call: 1-513-841-1722
Compatible general MIDI software.

SofTrax
Call: 1-214-709-7400
Compatible MIDI music for contemporary worship.

Worship Arrangements by Gracenote Inc.
Call: 1-403-413-1729
Fax: 1-403-418-1498
E-mail: gnote@compusmart.ab.ca
Individual songs include notated parts for vocals with harmonies, piano, synthesizer, guitar, bass, and drums. A lead sheet and full score are included with the CD. Songs include numerous chorus arrangements from Integrity and Mercy Publishing libraries, hymn standards, and Christmas carols.

Worship Media Resources
Call: 1-800-600-6334
Compatible general MIDI software.

Part 2

IMPLEMENTING
THE SERVICE

Chapter 6
Designing the Service

The Design Team

Who is the design team? At the very least, the pastor and director of worship are the team. Try to include a few more people on your team, whether they are church staff or volunteers. Several different creative ideas will always help. The pastor will speak from the preaching perspective and the musician will speak from the music perspective. But is that all there is to worship? Not in this case. We want to speak to the needs of the congregation, therefore a layperson who can help interpret these needs will be very helpful. A person who thinks in terms of today's media will add another dimension to your team. Try to include someone who is a walking encyclopedia of movies, television, and the Internet. You will be a giant step ahead!

Set a specific time each week to come together to create the service. We meet on Tuesday afternoon to plan the next Sunday's service. You may not always have the theme for the service before you begin planning, but try to give a scripture and possible theme to the design team a week or more before its use so the team's creative juices can already be at work. This will save time and reduce anxiety the week of the service.

How is a theme chosen? Many churches begin by following the lectionary. But you do not need to be completely tied to the lectionary when you feel led to address a specific cultural issue or congregational need. At these times, take a thematic approach to relate the cultural issue or congregational need to a scripture passage. Quite often a three- or four-week series will come from this theme.

1. Read the scripture text.

Begin the design team meeting by reading the scripture text from several different versions, including contemporary translations. Ask each person to listen carefully for predominant ideas. Then ask the team members to talk about how the scripture speaks to people today. How does it relate to our everyday lives? What is God's Word for us? How can we take the church to the hurting world? Will they listen? Will they hear?

2. Develop a theme from the Word.

If we can design a service that interprets the message in many different ways and gives the worshiper an opportunity to truly experience the Word, then the congregation will hear in ways they have never heard before. With this in mind, begin to develop a theme from the Word. Use secular media to relate a theme to contemporary life. Current trends reflect what people are thinking about, so use them! Get your ideas from movies, television shows, and commercials. Yes, I know they all seem to be sending the wrong message. I'm sure we could count on one hand the shows and commercials with Christian values. But if we are so inundated with the wrong messages that have become an accepted part of our lives, then what better way to teach God's Word than by comparing the two side by side? This will probably be a new style of preaching for your pastor and may be one that will be foreign to what was taught in seminary. Yet, this is what we need to hear because our culture is speaking in a foreign tongue. We need to know how God expects us to respond to today's world.

3. List ways to interpret the theme.

These include music, movie and television clips, drama, dance, visuals, altar, smells, touch, and taste. Begin with music, movie clips, and drama first, as they are the easiest to choose. But don't slight the others, for they can sometimes be the most powerful tools since they are not used as often. For example, you probably won't use dance every week, but when it is used, it will send a powerful visual message. And, you probably won't use smell that often, but when you bake bread during communion, the sense of smell will reinforce the experience of sharing a meal with Christ. (You will need a kitchen in close proximity or portable cooking device for this.) A sense of touch can be incorporated by giving the worshiper something to take home from the service as a reminder of the message. The altar (more information in chapter 7) and the computerized visual presentation are the obvious places to powerfully illustrate the theme. But don't forget that other objects can be used. (We used a full-size inflated rubber raft one Sunday to set the stage for Jesus' breakfast on the beach with the disciples. The scene was complete with oars, life jackets, fishing nets, and rubber fish.)

4. Make a list of components.

Remember that there is no formula for contemporary worship. Nothing says you have to take an offering, say the Lord's Prayer, or whatever your congregation is accustomed to doing. (I'm sure God won't strike you dead for not taking an offering, but the finance committee might!) The fewer components you have to worry about plugging in somewhere, the more creative you can be in designing a truly experiential worship service. I am not advocating eliminating the offering in contemporary services, but in each service it should reinforce the message of the day. You can have an offering taken every Sunday in the contemporary service, but try to do it in unique ways so that it does not break the flow of the service.

Think of creative ways to include these components in your service:

The Offering. Use it as a time to teach the importance of an offering and give meaning to the ritual.

The Scripture Reading. Show the scripture passage on a

video, act it out, have a dancer interpret the reading, write it in a lifestyle sketch, read it responsively, or simply use it as a part of the sermon.

The Prayer Time. Ask the congregation to share their praises and concerns verbally, write prayer request on slips of paper to bring to the altar, intersperse the prayers of the congregation throughout the sermon time, let the congregation pray with those sitting around them, or have several different types of prayers throughout the service.

The Communion Liturgy. If the sermon flows smoothly into communion, do not speak the Great Thanksgiving, for example—simply consecrate the elements with words or with motions only and serve. If your service is not over two hundred people, have twelve people come forward at a time and be seated at a table to be served. Have experienced mimes act out the liturgy of communion and then serve. Write your own modern-day liturgy.

Other Liturgy. You may choose to use a Call to Worship, a Litany, a Responsive Reading, an Affirmation of Faith, and/or a unison Benediction. This is your best opportunity to relate God's Word to today's world. Write your own liturgy in today's language so that it reflects the theme of the service and your congregational needs. There are some new resources to help you get started with this (see the Resource List).

Communicating Congregational Stories. This can be the sharing of personal faith stories (it always works better to use an interview format, as this helps to keep laypeople focused and within a time frame), a mission opportunity for the congregation to share in, or a personal story that relates to the theme.

Response to the Word. This can be done in many different ways to allow the worshiper time to reflect on what has been said: play meditative music in combination with beautiful scenes projected on the screen; have a special music presentation that reflects the spoken word; receive the offering; or think of something the people can actively do in response.

5. Make a list of music that fits the theme.

Include congregational songs, solos, special anthems, or praise band music. How can the music be used to bridge the components of the service and make one complete worship experience? Begin putting all the components together using the music as a bridge. Certainly the music will stand alone at some points of the service, but it will help the flow of the service if it is also used to tie it all together. Transitions from one component of worship to another should have a purpose. Don't just insert music as filler (what I like to call "traveling" music).

6. Time the service and type the script.

When I first began scripting services, I sat with a stopwatch at my desk and sang each song as it would be performed, so I could get an exact timing. Then I wrote all the dialogue for the worship leaders. I still script each service, but not with as much precise detail since we are all much more experienced. You might not like the idea of writing out everything to be said by the worship leaders, but I believe that it is needed in order to begin with the level of professionalism you will want for the service. If your worship leaders were recruited from within your congregation, they will be very grateful for this script. This will give them confidence in case words fail them suddenly. Leading a congregation in worship is much easier said than done. Often, it is difficult to remember song lyrics, instructions that need to be given (stand up, sit down, sing again), what to pray, and the order of the service when you are in front of a group of people.

The following are examples of four contemporary worship scripts. The first script is a good example of where you might begin. Give each praise team singer and band member a notebook with the script, all the music, and the necessary liturgy. Abbreviations can be used to simplify the script, for example: WL = worship leaders (the two up front); PT = praise team (singers and band); CTW = call to worship.

WORSHIP SCRIPT #1

Components
- Three songs of praise and thanksgiving
- Two songs of worship
- One prayer song and prayer time
- Announcements/greeting one another
- Children's time
- Two songs of preparation
- Scripture and sermon
- The offering as a response to the Word
- A time of commitment during the closing song
- Benediction

Service

8:30

WL: Welcome (memorized).

PT Singers: Read Psalm 100 from notebook (written to be read by the six singers).

WL: Have the congregation stand for the opening songs.
1. "I Will Enter His Gates" (2x)
2. "We Gather Together" (all 3 verses)
3. "We Bring the Sacrifice of Praise" (2x)

8:36

WL: "Please be seated as we continue to prepare our hearts for worship. Psalm 95 says, 'Come, let us bow down in worship, let us kneel before the Lord our Maker.' " (Read during introduction to the next song.)
4. "I Will Worship You, Lord" (2x)
5. "I Worship You, Almighty God" (2x)

8:39

WL: Read prayer in notebook during introduction to the next song.

    6. "Sanctuary" (2x)

(PT Singers are seated to the sides of the platforms.)

8:41

Pastor: Ask two ushers to come forward (with the cordless microphones) so the congregation will have the opportunity to share their praises and concerns. Then have a pastoral prayer, followed by the Lord's Prayer.

8:46

Pastor: Welcome and announcements. Ask the children to come forward for children's time as the people stand and greet one another.

8:49

WL: Lead children's time. As the children return to their seats, PT Singers rise to lead the songs of preparation.

    7. "Give Thanks" (once with optional ending)

    8. "In All Things" (2x)

9:01

Pastor: Scripture (Eph. 1:3-14) and sermon: "Leave Room!" (twenty minutes).

9:21

Pastor: Ask the ushers to come forward to receive the offering. Piano solo based on "Give Thanks" is played during the offering.

9:25

Pastor: Give an invitation to commitment. Ask people to stand for the closing song.

(PT up front.)

9. "Praise and Thanksgiving" (3 verses)

(Based on the hymn tune BUNESSAN—"Morning Has Broken.")

9:27

WL: Closing prayer (in notebook) and congregational response (on screen).

10. "Hallelujah, Amen!"

PT Band: "I Will Enter His Gates" (1x)

"We Bring the Sacrifice of Praise" (2x)

SOURCES

Come and Worship. Mobile, Ala.: Integrity Music, Inc., 1994. (A collection of two hundred popular songs for praise and worship.)

Songs for Praise and Worship. Nashville: Word Music, 1992.

The United Methodist Hymnal. Nashville: The United Methodist Publishing House, 1989.

The Upper Room Worshipbook. Nashville: The Upper Room, 1985.

WORSHIP SCRIPT #2

Components

- Welcome and announcements
- Two opening praise songs
- CTW #1 to establish the primary theme
- Two songs that relate to the theme
- CTW #2 to establish secondary theme

- One prayer song with congregational prayer time
- Instrumental interlude before a Mission Minute by layperson
- One song of preparation
- Scripture to be read and presented in a dramatic sketch
- Sermon
- Communion as the response to the Word
- Related music during communion
- Closing song and benediction

Service

8:30

Pastor: Welcome/announcements/congregational greetings.

PT Band: "I Will Celebrate" (1x)

PT Singers: (up front) "I Will Celebrate" (2x)
1. "I Will Celebrate"
2. "Sing and Be Glad in Him" (2x + D.C.)

WL: Lead CTW #1 in notebook and on screen.
3. "This Is My Commandment" (2x)
4. "Behold What Manner of Love" (2x)

WL: Seat congregation and lead CTW #2 in notebook and on screen.
5. "In Moments Like These" (PT 1x/all 1x)

8:50

(PT Singers seated on sides.)

Pastor: Lead congregational prayer time. End with instrumental prayer response.

8:55

(Mission Minute speaker comes forward during the prayer response.)

9:00

(PT Singers up front to lead song of preparation.)
    6. "With All My Heart" (2x)

Sound Operator: Reads 1 Corinthians 13:1-3 from the back while the pastor removes four items (cymbals, books, mountain, jewelry box) from the altar.

9:03

PT: Begins sketch: "What Love Is Not" with song in discord (see sketch at the end of this script).
    7. "I Love You, Lord" (singers in F/instruments in G for a few measures only)

(All PT members come to the platform to play their part in the sketch.)
    Finish the sketch with "I Love You, Lord" (2x) while the pastor completes the altar (banner, light candles, communion elements).

9:13

Pastor: Sermon: "The Mirror of Love"

9:20

Time of Communion: Served by intinction.
    Solo: "The Gift of Love"
(At the end of communion, the pastor will offer a time of commitment.)

9:25

(PT up front to lead closing song.)
    8. "They'll Know We Are Christians" (verses 1, 3-4)

Pastor: Benediction

PT Band: "I Will Celebrate" (1x)

CALL TO WORSHIP #1 (on screen)
WL#1: Love circles around,
People: Joining hands, linking hearts
WL#2: Flowing from parent to child,
People: From friend to friend to friend;
WL#1: From one beloved to another.
People: Love circles around,
WL#2: Never giving up,
People: Always reaching out.
WL#1: Love circles around,
People: And God's love embraces all.

From *Sourcebook of Worship Resources*, Vol. 2 (Canton, Ohio: Communication Resources, Inc.), p. 26.

CALL TO WORSHIP #2 (on screen)
WL#1: In Christ, we are made new
People: And filled with hope.
WL#2: In God, we belong to a new community,
People: Discovering we are friends, sisters and brothers in Christ.
WL#1: In Christ, the old ways have lost their glitter and appeal,
People: For we have turned toward the new light.
WL#2: In God, we receive a new name and a new call;
People: We are God's beloved, and we carry on the ministry of reconciliation.

WL#1: In Christ, we are a new creation.

People: The old is passed away, and we live as signs of reconciliation and love.

From *Sourcebook of Worship Resources,* Vol. 2 (Canton, Ohio: Communication Resources, Inc.), p. 28.

WL#1: Let us pray. Holy God, we rejoice that you have made us in love and for love. You love us so much that your forgiveness is unlimited and yet we count how many times we have been wronged. You love us so much that you chose to die for us and yet we consider it an inconvenience to take time out of our busy schedule to be fully present with someone else for a few minutes. We need your love because our love is so small. Holy God, refashion us in love and for love so that all our relationships are marked with love, joy, and peace. Amen.

Sketch

(After a few measures of singing out of tune, the first PT member speaks up.)

PT Member #1: Come on guys, can't we get this thing right? Honestly, sometimes I wonder where your brains are. It's not that difficult! I think a third-grader could do it.

Pastor: *(Strikes big gong. Reads 1 Corinthians 13:4a.)* "Love is patient and kind."

PT Member #2: If I would have been singing lead this wouldn't have happened! I don't know why the director doesn't let me sing lead every week. She knows I'm the only one who can do it right!

Pastor: *(Strikes big gong. Reads 1 Corinthians 13:4b.)* "Love is not jealous or boastful."

PT Member #3: Well, excuse me! I thought I was doing just fine! But the drummer, well, you know drummers! Why do they have such an attitude?

Pastor: *(Strikes big gong. Reads 1 Corinthians 13:5a.)* "Love is not arrogant or rude."

PT Member #4: I just can't play in this key! I tell the director every week that it has to be in the key of D, but does she listen to me? If she's not going to put it in my key then I will just take my guitar and go home!

Pastor: *(Strikes big gong. Reads 1 Corinthians 13:5b.)* "Love does not insist on its own way."

PT Member #5: *(To the director.)* Why do you always have to have your way? You are such a perfectionist! Everyone resents singing for you because it's never good enough!

Pastor: *(Strikes big gong. Reads 1 Corinthians 13:5c.)* "Love is not irritable or resentful."

PT Member #6: I knew this wasn't going to work out! I told you so, but did you listen to me?

Pastor: *(Strikes gong. Reads 1 Corinthians 13:6.)* "Love does not rejoice in wrong." *(Continues to read through verse 8.)*

SOURCES

Hymns for the Family of God. Nashville: Paragon Association, Inc., 1976.

Praise and Worship Songbook 6. Mobile, Ala.: Integrity Music, Inc., 1992.

Songs for Praise and Worship. Nashville: Word Music, 1992.

WORSHIP SCRIPT #3

Components
- Welcome and announcements
- CTW to introduce songs
- Three opening songs
- Two worship songs
- Two prayer songs
- Congregational prayer time
- Mission Minute
- Offering
- Children's time
- One song of preparation
- Scripture in dramatic form
- Sermon
- Time of reflection using theme song
- Closing song and benediction

Service
8:30

Pastor: Welcome/announcements/congregational greetings.

PT Band: "In Him We Live" (1x + coda song ending)

(PT Singers up front during prelude.)

8:35

WL: Have the congregation stand and lead the CTW in notebook and on screen.
  1. "In Him We Live" (2x + coda ending)
  2. "Awesome Power" (2x + segue)
  3. "Awesome God" (3x + song ending)

WL: Introduce the worship songs.
  4. "Open Our Eyes, Lord" (2 vss.)
  5. "As the Deer" (3 vss.)

WL: Introduce the prayer songs.
  6. "Change My Heart, O God" (1x + segue)
  7. "In My Life, Lord, Be Glorified" (2x in C/1x in D)

8:45
(PT Singers seated on sides)

Pastor: Lead congregational prayer.

8:50
(Mission Minute person comes forward during the instrumental prayer response.)

8:55

Pastor: Asks the ushers to come forward to receive the offering.

PT Band: "Lord, You Have Come to the Lakeshore"

8:58

Pastor: Ask the children to come forward. Explain what it might have been like to have breakfast on the beach with Jesus. The children pass out paper fish (previously made) to everyone in the congregation.

9:05

(PT Singers up front to lead song of preparation.)
    8. "Lord, You Have Come to the Lakeshore"

PT: Perform scripture reading (Luke 5:1-11) in notebook, then be seated out front.

9:10

Pastor: Sermon: "Let's Go Fishing" (fifteen minutes).

9:25

Time of reflection:
(PT Singers up front to lead closing song.)
"Lord, You Have Come to the Lakeshore"

Pastor: Benediction

PT Band: "In Him We Live" (1x)

CALL TO WORSHIP (on screen)

WL#1: This is the day the Lord has made. Clap your hands—raise a joyful shout to God.

People: For our God is awesome and reigns over all the earth.

WL#2: How good it is to give thanks and sing to you, most high God;

People: To proclaim your constant love every morning and your faithfulness every night;

WL#1: Sing out your joy to the Creator.

People: Let us praise our God.

Scripture Reading (Luke 5:1-11 NRSV)
(Assign these parts to PT members: Narrator, Simon, Jesus.)

Narrator: Once while Jesus was standing beside the lake of Gennesaret, and the crowd was pressing in on him to hear the word of God, he saw two boats there at the shore of the lake; the fishermen had gone out of them and were washing their nets. He got into one of the boats, the one belonging to Simon, and asked him to put out a little way from the shore. Then he sat down and taught the crowds from the boat. When he had finished speaking, he said to Simon,

Jesus: "Put out into the deep water and let down your nets for a catch."

Narrator: Simon answered,

Simon: "Master, we have worked all night long but have caught nothing. Yet if you say so, I will let down the nets."

Narrator: When they had done this, they caught so many fish that their nets were beginning to break. So they signaled their partners in the other boat to come and help them. And they came and filled both boats, so that they began to sink. But when Simon Peter saw it, he fell down at Jesus' knees, saying,

Simon: "Go away from me, Lord, for I am a sinful man!"

Narrator: For he and all who were with him were amazed at the catch of fish that they had taken; and so also were James and John, sons of Zebedee, who were partners with Simon. Then Jesus said to Simon,

Jesus: "Do not be afraid; from now on you will be catching people."

Narrator: When they had brought their boats to shore, they left everything and followed him.

SOURCES

Songs for Praise and Worship. Nashville: Word Music, 1992.

The United Methodist Hymnal. Nashville: The United Methodist Publishing House, 1989.

WORSHIP SCRIPT #4

Components
- Welcome/congregational greetings/lead into theme of service
- One opening song
- CTW
- Two songs (God as sole provider)
- Invocation
- One song to bring worshipers into God's presence
- Pastoral prayer
- Offering
- Sermon
- Congregational prayer (worshipers write prayers on slips of paper)
- Response to the Word (worshipers come forward to burn the slips of paper)
- Closing song
- Benediction

8:30

Pastor: Welcome and congregational greetings. Lead into the theme: "What's Possessing You?"

(PT up front during introduction.)

WL: Have congregation stand for song.
   1. "Arise and Sing" (2x)

WL: Lead CTW in notebook.
   2. "He Is Jehovah" (3 verses)
   3. "Jehovah-Jireh" (2x)

8:40

WL: Seat the congregation. Read the invocation in notebook during the introduction to the next song.
   4. "Only by Grace" (as written)

Pastor: Short prayer, then ask the ushers to come forward for the offering.
   5. "Jesus Is My Lord" (2x)

8:45

Pastor: Sermon: "What's Possessing You?" (slide presentation)
   Luke 8:26-39 is first set up by reading the scripture and describing some of the things that possess us. Then there are four segments that are listed on the screen and on the worshiper's sheet for taking notes. (1) "Indiana Jones "movie clip; (2) "Remember Your Chains," song by Steven Curtis Chapman; (3) "Pretty Proud of It," Cross Point script (#12410) by Dave McClellan; and (4) Life Styles visual.

Segment #1: *Materialism.* Show "Indiana Jones" clip.

Segment #2: *Addictions.* Play taped song "Remember Your Chains" with coordinated picture slides.

Segment #3: *Pride.* Praise Team up front for skit: "Pretty Proud of It."

Segment #4: *Life Styles.* Pastor questions the person who has been chained to a chair in front of the altar.

9:15
Pastor: Lead congregational prayer time.

9:20
Response to the Word
People come forward to drop their "possessions" (written on pieces of paper) in a bucket. (A galvanized bucket is sitting on the floor in front of the person chained to the chair.) Then the papers are set on fire. *(WARNING! Make sure your smoke detectors or sprinkler system will not go off. Place a fireproof liner under the bucket.)*

(PT up front to lead the closing song.)
6. "He Whom the Son Sets Free" (as written)

Pastor: Benediction is given as a part of untying the person chained to the chair.

PT Band: "Arise and Sing" (1x)

CALL TO WORSHIP (on screen)
WL: Ever-present God, forever seeking us and always teaching us:
People: Open our minds to the truth of your care.
WL: Open our hearts to the gentle caress of your love.
People: Open our lips to share stories of faith.
WL: Open our hands to create beauty, do justice and show kindness.

People: Open our souls to the breath of your Spirit.

WL: Open our mouths to sing boldly and loudly your praises.

People: Amen!

From *Sourcebook for Worship Resources Vol. 2* (Canton, Ohio: Communication Resources, Inc.), p. 55.

INVOCATION

Lord God,

Full of compassion and gracious,

Long-suffering and overflowing with mercy and truth:

Turn to us, and give us grace.

Show us the signs of your good pleasure.

Let us rejoice in the light of your presence.

Magnify your name among us, O Lord. Amen

From *Sourcebook for Worship Resources Vol. 2* (Canton, Ohio: Communication Resources, Inc.), p. 56.

SOURCES

Come and Worship. Mobile, Ala.: Integrity Music, Inc., 1994.

Praise and Worship Songbook 6. Mobile, Ala.: Integrity Music, Inc., 1992.

Songs for Praise and Worship. Nashville: Word Music, 1992

Bulletins or Not?

When we began our contemporary service, we designed a new style of bulletin and used it for nine months. During the summer we decided to do without a bulletin. That was one of the best decisions we made! If you opt to go without bulletins, people may complain at first. The trained "churchgoer" may be disturbed by not knowing what is coming next. On the other hand, seekers do not necessarily understand the "churchy" terminology used in the bulletin, and will not have any preconceived notions about what should take place next in the order of worship. The greatest benefit to having no bulletin is the anticipation of what is next. The worshiper is much more engaged in the service, will listen and watch more carefully, and therefore, will be more able to participate. Also, there is no reason to look down, so eyes are always up! Everything is on screen: announcements, names of PT participants, titles and composers of any special music, special speakers, title of the sermon, and so on. Of course if you are not using video projection, you will need a bulletin to cover all of these items.

But what about announcements? A high-tech, attractive brochure about your church and its ministries could be handed out to visitors. You will want to get information about what your church offers in their hands immediately. Some churches choose to print weekly announcements in a handout form so that a tear-off registration of attendance and a prayer request form can be included.

The following is an example of the bulletin format we used at Munsey.

Munsey Memorial United Methodist
Contemporary Worship
October 13, 1996
Sunday 8:30 A.M.   Fellowship Hall

- Songs of Praise   "How Majestic Is Your Name"
  "To God Be the Glory"

- Call to Worship   "I Was Glad When They Said Unto Me"

- Time of Prayer
  Sharing Our Praises and Concerns
  The Lord's Prayer
  Prayer Response: "Open Our Eyes, Lord"

- Time of Sharing and Greeting   "We Are an Offering"

- Stewardship Moment   "Give Thanks"

- Scripture Presentation

- Sermon   "What Did Jesus See?"
  Al Bowles, Senior Pastor

- Responding to God
  Offering: "Freely, Freely"

- Closing Prayer and Response   "Hallelujah, Amen!"

Welcome to Munsey
Expect an encounter with the living Christ!

The Lord's Prayer
Our Father in heaven,
       hallowed be your name
       your kingdom come,
       your will be done, on earth as in heaven.
Give us today our daily bread.
Forgive us our sins
       as we forgive those who have sinned against us.
Save us from the time of trial,
       and deliver us from evil.
For the kingdom, the power, and the glory are yours,
       now and forever. Amen.

Today's Scripture
Mark 12:41-44
(New Revised Standard Version)

He sat down opposite the treasury, and watched the crowd putting money into the treasury. Many rich people put in large sums. A poor widow came and put in two small copper coins, which are worth a penny. Then he called his disciples and said to them, "Truly I tell you, this poor widow has put in more than all those who are contributing to the treasury. For all of them have contributed out of their abundance; but she out of her poverty has put in everything she had, all she had to live on."

Worship Participants

PREACHER	Al Bowles
WORSHIP LEADERS	Jerry Hurst, Lynn Hurst
SINGERS	Bryan Long, Diane Short,
	Daryl Stephens, Linda Perry
SYNTHESIZER	Ann O'Quinn
DRUMMER	Ryan Stanton
GUITARS	Marcus Ledbetter, Derek Osborne
FLUTE	Diane Short
SOUND/VIDEO TECHNICIANS	Jennifer Ledbetter, Doug Miller
SCRIPTURE PRESENTER	Beverly Dugger

Joining the Munsey Family

(If you wish to place your membership with Munsey Church this morning, please complete the following and bring it to the front during the final song. We are glad to have you!)

Name _____

Children's Name(s) _____

Transferring From _____

Profession of Faith _____

(Please join the following response as we accept this morning's new members.)

Pastor: Brothers and sisters, I commend to your love and care these persons whom we this day receive into the membership of this congregation. Do all in your power to increase their faith, confirm their hope, and perfect them in love.

Congregation: We rejoice to recognize you as members of Christ's holy church, and bid you welcome to the Munsey Congregation of The United Methodist Church. With you we renew our vows to uphold it by our prayers, our presence, our gifts and our service. With God's help we will so order our lives after the example of Christ that, surrounded by steadfast love, you may be established in the faith and confirmed and strengthened in the way that leads to life eternal.

Requests

I would like information on:

❑ Sunday school classes
❑ Children's activities
❑ Youth activities
❑ Singles' activities
❑ Women's activities

❑ Men's activities
❑ Music activities
❑ Bible studies
❑ Counseling ministries
❑ Would like to receive the newsletter

Comments, Requests, or Prayer Needs:

Mr./Mrs./Ms. _____

Address _____

City _____ State _____ Zip _____

Telephone _____

SERMON NOTES
What Did Jesus See? Mark 12:41-44

INTRODUCTION
A. What was there about the nameless widow that caught the attention of Jesus?

B. What was it about the poor widow's last penny, which she put in the Temple treasury, that made it a fortune in the eyes of Jesus?

C. Her two copper coins tell of a gift of love and gratitude.

OUTLINE
1. An Act of Worship

2. An Affirmation of Faith

3. A Desire to Be Involved in Multiplying God's Love

4. A Recognition of Her Spiritual Need to Give

CONCLUSION:
What story does your giving tell Jesus about you?

CHECKLIST #6: DESIGNING THE SERVICE

- Who will be on the design team?
- When will the team meet?
- Develop a theme for the service.
- List ways to interpret the theme.
- List necessary components of the service.
- List all possible music for the service.
- Write bridges and transitions, and time all components.
- Type scripts for all involved.
- Decide on an order of worship bulletin or an announcement/registration page.

RESOURCE LIST

Books

Cathy Townley and Mike Graham, *Come Celebrate! A Guide for Planning Contemporary Worship.* Nashville: Abingdon Press, 1995. (A workbook with video cassette included.)

Lisa Flinn and Barbara Younger. *Creative Ways to Offer Praise: 100 Ideas for Sunday Worship.* Nashville: Abingdon Press, 1993. Includes visual touches, sharing sermons, Holy Communion and fellowship foods, worship mementos.

Drama Resources

Drama for Worship, Volumes 1-8
Distributed by Word, Inc.
Call: 1-800-251-4000

The Worship Drama Library
Lillenas Publishing Co.
Kansas City, MO 64101
Nine volumes with twelve dramas each; listed by topic. Permission to copy for local use.

Cross Point Scripts Vol. I. Canton, Ohio: Communication Resources, 1997.

Communication Resources
4150 Belden Village St., N.W.
Canton, Ohio 44718
Call: 1-800-98-DRAMA
Fax: 1-330-493-7897
E-mail: drama@comresources.com
Internet: www.dramaministry.com

Fifty scripts, including three- to seven-minute dramatic sketches, readers theater and mime; indexed by scripture text and related topics/themes.

Worship Resources

Homiletics
Internet: www.HomileticsOnline.com
E-mail: order@comresources.com

Magazine or online subscription published bimonthly. Includes: commentary on a selected text; ideas for developing a sermon; a children's sermon; related hymn and song suggestions; worship resources.

The Power of Teams
Ginghamsburg United Methodist Church
6759 South County Rd. 25-A
Tipp City, Ohio
Call: 1-937-667-1069
Fax: 1-937-667-5677

How-to video on the use of teams for designing worship.

Sourcebook for Worship Resources, Vol. II
Communication Resources, Inc.
Call: 1-800-992-2144
Fax: 1-330-493-3158
E-mail: order@comresources.com

Sunday Morning Live from Willow Creek Community Church, ed. Steve Peterson

  Willow Creek Resources/Zondervan
  Call: 1-800-876-7335
  Fax: 1-610-532-9001
  Internet: www.zondervan.com
Each volume includes six reproducible sketches. Video of each is available.

Worship Software (for Windows)
A worship planning resource that includes: a comprehensive listing of 5,000+ songs; songs cross-referenced by key, theme, time signature, scripture reference, tempo, and usage history; an event calendar for scheduling events, locations, people and music; a program for designing and printing customized bulletins and programs; and much more.

Videos

  Gospel Films Video Catalog
  Gospel Films, Inc.
  P.O. Box 455
  Muskegon, MI 49443-0455
  Call: 1-800-253-0413
  Fax: 1-616-777-1847
  Internet: www.gospelcom.nte/catalog
  Includes software, books, and internet resources.

  21st Century Ministries Church Media Kit
  Call: 1-800-748-5119
A wonderful guide to video clips; indexed by subjects and gives the exact frames to use.

Chapter 7
The Design
of the Worship Space

Setting the Mood

The first impression a worshiper receives upon entering the worship space will always be the most important. A mood should be set and the theme well depicted to invite the person to worship. What does your space say? Is it the same basic altar every week? Is there anything about the room that sets the mood?

When we began our contemporary service, we purchased only a few items for the altar. Now we have an altar closet full of: materials, netting, assorted candleholders and candles, silk ivy, pottery, and a water fountain, along with many more unusual items. Creating unique altar designs has been one of the least expensive components of worship, but one of the most rewarding for the designer, pastor, and congregation.

Begin by considering how the theme of the service can be depicted. Write down any idea, no matter how far-fetched it may seem. Decide if there should be one item that is the focal point on the altar or if there should be several items. Remember that there are no rules to break in this service. There does not have to be a cross or two or three candles and a Bible on the altar at every service. It is preferable, though, to display a cross prominently somewhere in the room, if not on the altar.

The following are some suggested ideas:

For the Worship Script #2 service described in the previous chapter, specific items can be used on the altar to depict the scripture, 1 Corinthians 13. Instead of an altar cloth, hang a white banner embellished with a red heart from the center of the table. Place a twenty-four-inch mirror in the center of the altar with three white candles in front of the mirror. The candles are symbolic of faith, hope, and love, so the love candle should be taller and placed in the middle. Starting at the left of the table and moving to the right place objects on the altar to depict the scripture reading. As the scripture is read, remove the appropriate items. Suggested items are a cymbal; a stack of books (knowledge); a mountain (made from plastic foam); and an elaborate gold jewelry box. Place a large Chinese gong on the floor next to the altar to be used during the skit "What Love Is Not." At the conclusion of the skit, the communion elements (bread and two cups of juice) can be brought forward and the candles lighted to prepare the table. As people come to the table for communion, they first see themselves in the mirror—a concluding point to the sermon: God is seen in you.

For the Worship Script #3 service, the entire room can depict the theme rather than only focusing on the altar. Move the altar table to the left of the platforms, slightly off-center. Place a cloth made from potato sack fabric on the altar. Black felt cutouts depicting Jesus and his disciples fishing from a boat can be added to the cloth. A fishing net is thrown over the side of the boat. Add the words "Come, follow me" to the cloth. Place a small fish tank with a large goldfish in the center of the altar. On either side of the fish tank place iron candleholders in the shape of fish. To the right of the altar have a fully inflated, adult-sized rubber raft with oars and life jackets leaning against the raft. Hang yellow and orange fishing nets on the altar, the rubber raft, and the music stands on the platforms.

For the Worship Script #4 service, drape a large piece of muslin fabric on the altar. Place a tall, black, wrought iron, triple candleholder in the middle. Use three medium-sized, ivory pillar candles in the holder. Drape a heavy twelve-foot metal chain over the muslin fabric. A fifty-foot hemp rope hangs over and around the table, so that the altar appears completely bound. Place a galvanized bucket on the floor in front of the altar with a six-foot chain around it. Use the bucket at the conclusion of the sermon for the worshipers to place their pieces of paper to be burned. Remember to place something under the bucket if you plan to burn the papers!

Here are other ideas for creative designs:

- Have the praise team process with the items to be placed on the altar.
- Create an Old Testament altar with fabrics, pottery, and wicker baskets.
- Create a Mission Sunday or Worldwide Communion Sunday altar with multicolor blankets, a world globe, mini flags from countries around the world, and baskets.
- Pentecost can be beautifully depicted with a white dove (found in craft stores) placed in a descending position on a cross. Use a red cloth on the altar and either red or white netting descending from above and behind the cross down to the floor.
- Use oil lamps or three-wick candles on occasion.
- Balloon bouquets are nice on special occasions (Pentecost, Rally Day, and anniversary of service). Create a bouquet that is approximately seven to eight feet above the floor and place it next to the altar.
- Drape fabric around potted flower arrangements: chrysanthemums in fall colors for October; poinsettias for Christmas; and lilies for Easter.

These are suggested items to have in your basic altar "pantry":

1. Six to ten yards of fabrics in liturgical colors (white, purple, green, and red). Use quality polyester that will not wrinkle and will drape well. Try to purchase this when the fabric store is having a sale or talk with the manager to see if you can get a special discount for your church. Consider adding aqua-colored fabric to use as the symbol of water, and black fabric for Good Friday or the beginning of your Easter service. These fabrics can be used as filler around objects on the altar, as a part of the design, or as flowing connectors from the altar to the congregation.

2. *Tulle (extra fine net).* Tulle is wonderful to work with in designing an altar. You will not want to use it every week, but it will add a beautiful dimension to your design on occasion. The cost of tulle is about one-fourth the price of comparable woven fabrics. I recommend purchasing ten yards of white, red, and aqua. Do not place tulle too close to lighted candles—it ignites easily!

3. *Candles in different sizes, shapes, and colors.* Purchase as many candles as your budget will allow. Large pillar candles can be used without holders. Look for sale prices at craft stores, department stores, or specialty stores. Try to find a few unusual candleholders—especially the type that hold three candles (Trinity). It is helpful to have candleholders of various styles: gold finish, black iron, and earthenware.

4. *Wicker baskets.* Baskets in different sizes and shapes and glass bowls for floating candles or baptismal water are useful on special occasions. Shop for these at craft and pottery stores.

5. *Silk ivy, ferns, and filler.* Artificial greenery can be rather expensive, but it adds so much to the creation of a complete design. Plants will be used quite often and are, therefore, well worth the expense.

6. *Other unusual items.* Collect sticks from yards, rocks from a river bottom, seashells, and any other items you think might be used. You never know what will spark your creativity!

After you have created your altar; look at it from all areas of the room. Then focus on the rest of the worship space. Is there anything that can be added to the room to create a special mood? You don't want to overdo the design, but sometimes a few simple items, placed strategically, can add a lot to the mood. After several Sundays of elaborate altars that depict the theme well, it is nice to have a simple but elegant altar one Sunday. The congregation will also appreciate this. The altar design can be so powerful that many worshipers (the visual learners) will be drawn into the service in greater depth because of it. Use this powerful tool and be blessed by it.

CHECKLIST #7: THE DESIGN OF THE WORSHIP SPACE
- A cross
- Altar cloths
- Polyester fabric in several colors
- Tulle in several colors
- Candles in several sizes and shapes
- Candleholders in different styles
- Wicker baskets, pottery, and glass bowls
- Silk plants
- A collection of unusual items
- A person or persons to design it

Chapter 8
The Rehearsal

How to Create Your Own Style

The rehearsal will be the place where you begin to develop and train musicians, and continually evolve your style and sound for worship. Most often, the musicians you have recruited from your church will be accustomed to performing hymns and anthems. They have probably not had experience in playing from a standard lead/chord chart with only chord symbols and an indication of the style (e.g., rock, R & B, Latin). Not all styles will fit your church, but keep in mind that you will want to use as many styles as possible in order to avoid the generic worship band sound week after week. The change in styles will broaden your worship experience.

The instruments of the rhythm section (piano/keyboard, guitar, bass guitar, and drums) will establish the style. The drums and bass guitar provide the foundational rhythmic elements. The keyboard and guitar provide the melody and harmonics.

The Drummer

The role of the drummer is to keep the rhythm steady for the band while also creating a style. The drummer must listen closely to the bass player. There is usually a similarity in what the bass drum and bass guitar play. Since much of what is played by these two will be improvised, it is important that they learn to play off each other and coordinate their efforts.

Drummers, of course, can make or break the band in several ways. They have the widest dynamic range possible of all instruments. The drummer should be willing to fall within the dynamic range that is needed for each particular song. The drummer should never be allowed to overpower the band, but should be expected to help keep the band together, especially when the band may be headed for a train wreck! This will take a lot of insistence from the director and willingness from the drummer to be a "part" of the whole unit, not the star soloist.

The Bass Guitarist

Some bass players are guitarists who have been willing to adapt to the bass since the instruments are so similar. The problem with this occurs when the player continues to play the bass in the same manner as the guitar. The bass is exactly that—the foundation of the chord/harmony. Therefore, the bass guitarist will usually play only one note at a time.

The bass player needs to understand three types of chord symbols:

1. Root position chords. One symbol is all that is needed. (See example below.) The bass guitarist plays the letter as shown. It will be the root of the chord.

2. Inverted chords. Since the chord is not in root position, the bass note will be indicated after a slash mark. (See example below.) In an inversion, the bass note will always be one of the notes of the chord. The bass player will play the letter to the right of the slash while the guitarists play the chord to the left of the slash.

3. Polychords. The bass player will still play the note to the

Sample music from "The Search," Come Celebrate! Jesus!, p. 61

MUSIC by Nylea L. Butler-Moore
© 1994 Abingdon Press

right of the slash although it will not be a note that belongs to the chord on the left side of the slash. (See example on previous page.) Also notice that polychords sometimes are written on top of each other. In this case, the bass player will play the note on the bottom and the guitarist will play the chord on top.

The bass can also be very effective as a solo instrument. When this takes place, it will be necessary for other instruments to assume the role of the foundation.

The Guitarist

The guitar is used mainly for the purpose of chording (also called "comping") and for improvised solos. The guitar can be used effectively when:

- doubling other instruments
- playing background melodies and fills
- playing the melody of a song
- playing improvised solos

There are other popular effects that your guitarists will probably be more than happy to use:

- Distortion (gives strength and energy to the sound but must be used with discretion)
- Choruses and delays (adds color to the sound but can be too "affected")
- Volume pedal (the player can control the volume with the foot and can also create swells as the volume is increased)

Most guitarists will be capable of following a chord chart. This should be a requirement before playing with the band in worship. The worship band needs to be polished enough to give support at all times to the singers and congregation. Anything less would be a distraction to worship.

The Keyboardist/Pianist

The keyboardist or pianist (interchangeable names) usually falls into one of two categories: classically trained or self-taught. There are certain strengths and weaknesses in each. While the traditionally trained pianist will probably have good sight-reading skills and technical flexibility, this person may not be able to read a standard lead/chord chart. The self-taught keyboardist will probably be adept at reading chord charts and playing by ear (improvising), but will not be able to deal with difficult score reading. If you have a keyboardist who can do it all, you are extremely blessed!

The traditional pianist is accustomed to playing the role of the entire rhythm section—flowing arpeggios in the right hand and heavy, powerful octaves in the left. This will not blend well when other instruments of the rhythm section are included. Therefore, the keyboardist needs to learn to play fewer notes. Pianists who want to play as many notes as possible will need to learn a new style of playing. The pianist's purpose is to provide harmonic support for the worship leaders and congregation, not to play as usual and let the other instruments fill in as they can. The overall sound should be orchestrated so that each instrument performs a vital role. Every instrument needs to stay focused on what the other instruments are playing and how all the parts fit together.

The electronic keyboard or acoustic piano will usually be the lead instrument, but the keyboardist should not carry all the parts. This is a difficult concept for most pianists to grasp, so it cannot be stated enough. If you use a traditionally trained pianist, encourage him or her to work on the skill of improvising in different styles from a chord chart. If you use a self-taught pianist, encourage him or her to work on the skill of SATB score reading. With practice and determination, each player can accomplish these goals.

As you begin your work with the band, be sure you know each player's individual abilities and experience. It will be helpful in leading them if you know their strengths and weaknesses as musicians. The best place to start is by listening to professional recordings of praise bands. Analyze what each instrument is playing as well as how each instrument fits with all the others. Make notations of what you hear in order to incorporate the technique into your band.

The pop/rock style is the foundation of most contemporary music. Understanding the principles of pop/rock is essential. With that as your foundation, it will be easier to develop other styles (e.g., ballads, country, gospel, Latin, funk/R&B) by introducing new rhythmic and harmonic developments. Explaining each of these styles would be too lengthy for this book. But do not fear, traditional musicians, there are some wonderful resources written just for you by Bob Barrett, director of music at Saddleback Church in California. These three resources will enable the classical musician to better understand a pop/rock style and learn how to orchestrate for a praise band. All of these books come with an accompanying CD-ROM.

The first book, *Contemporary Music Styles,* will develop those musicians whom God has called to be a part of their church's worship team. Also, with a better understanding of the fundamentals of contemporary music and a working knowledge of the many different musical styles, church musicians will be prepared for more opportunities to minister through music and will be more effective in leading their congregations in worship.

The second book, *Synthesizers in Praise and Worship,* will help the music director learn to build orchestral arrangements through electronic means that previously would not have been possible without an orchestra at his or her disposal.

The third book, *Reading and Writing Chords,* will help the director assist musicians in rehearsing and playing contemporary styles of music in worship.

(See Resource List at the end of the chapter for more information on these books.)

Here are a few ideas that will help you get started:

1. Choose music that has orchestrated parts for the praise band in separate editions—this will require that your musicians be able to read music, but it will be an excellent way to begin with a quality approach rather than a play-as-you-want approach.

2. If you are creating your own arrangements, try the layered method—introduce one or two instruments at a time to allow the music and style to build.

3. Decrease the sound by one or two instruments at a time.

4. Play the song in tempo throughout—this means giving rhythm to chord changes.

5. Play with *rubato*—this means that the drummer doesn't play except for some coloring while other instruments are sustaining half or whole notes.

6. As soon as possible, add other solo instruments, such as flute, saxophone, or brass to your band.

The Singers

Not every person who wants to be a singer in the praise team should. The singers should be able to learn and carry individual parts on their own. It is possible to use persons who do not read music, but their ability to improvise by ear must be strong. The singers should be able to clearly hear the chord structure and be able to harmonize within that structure.

When introducing a new song to the congregation, all singers should sing the melody. This will help the congregation hear what they will sing without hearing other parts that might confuse them. If the song is very easy to "catch," the praise team might sing the melody in unison only two times and then add in the parts on the third time through. If it is a medium-to-difficult song to remember, the praise team should sing only in unison. Vocal parts could be added the next time that you use the song in a service.

Use many different methods to teach new songs to the congregation. Some suggested methods: (1) have the band play the song as a prelude or offertory; (2) have a praise team member sing it as a solo; (3) have the praise team perform it as special music; or (4) use it as an opening and closing song or at least in two different places in the service.

At our weekly rehearsals, we rehearse only for the upcoming Sunday with the praise team that will be used. One way to facilitate this rehearsal is to rehearse for forty-five minutes with the band and then add the singers for the last forty-five minutes. The singers could have a separate rehearsal the first forty-five minutes if there is another leader. The entire praise team comes together once every four to eight weeks to learn new music and share together for team building.

The Contemporary Worship Music Library

Your library for contemporary music will probably look totally different from your traditional music library. Most of the service music is congregational so it is advisable to decide on one main book of praise songs. It will not be necessary to purchase congregational songbooks if you will be projecting the words onto a screen. Purchase a singer's edition for each of your praise team singers and the appropriate edition for each of your instrumentalists (if available). Each person will have his or her own copy at home with which to practice. For rehearsal and worship, provide a complete notebook of music, liturgy, and script for all praise team members so they will not have to flip through their books before each song. This will require weekly clerical help—an excellent job for a lay volunteer who desires to be a part of the ministry. Here is a suggested process for organizing the music:

1. Make one copy from the singer's edition; print your CCLI number at the bottom of the page; make six copies and mark with a red pen in the upper right corner WL, S, A, T, B, and M

(master). This will be legal if songbooks have been purchased for each of the singers.

2. Do the same for the instrumentalists, marking each copy with D (drum), BG (bass guitar), G (guitar), KB (keyboard), or S (synthesizer), and so on.

3. Set up one file cabinet drawer for singer's copies, one for instrumental copies, and one for keyboard/synthesizer copies.

4. Every week after the scripts are typed and copied, have someone put together the notebooks needed for Sunday's praise team. On Monday, the notebooks are refiled. This is an easy routine that is not very time-consuming unless you get behind in filing.

CHECKLIST #8: THE REHEARSAL

- Study the pop/rock style.
- Listen to recordings of praise bands.
- Begin learning how to orchestrate for the praise band.
- Plan your rehearsal structure.
- Create a system for a contemporary worship music library.
- Create praise team notebooks or something similar.

RESOURCE LIST

Bob Barrett. *Contemporary Music Styles: The Worship Band's Guide to Excellence*. Mission Viejo, Calif.: Taylor Made Music Publishing, 1996. Call: 1-949-457-1892 to order.

———. *Reading and Writing Chords: The Music Director's Guide to Communicating with the Band*. Mission Viejo, Calif.: Taylor Made Music Publishing, 1998.

———. *Synthesizers in Praise and Worship: The Worship Band's Guide to Excellence*. Mission Viejo, Calif.: Taylor Made Music Publishing, 1997.

Chapter 9
Advertising

You will certainly want to get the word out about your new service. There are a lot of different ways to do this and a wide range of costs. First, look into every avenue available to you, then evaluate the costs and projected effectiveness before making a decision. It is assumed that you will be communicating with your congregation through the pulpit and church newsletter about all details leading to the new worship service. Most of the ideas here are for advertising outside the church.

1. Hire a professional advertising agency to develop a campaign for your new worship service. This is like hiring a sound consultant as described in chapter 2. If you have the budget, go for it! As with any business, check their references and work. Do they work well with their clients? Do they meet deadlines and budgets? Know your budget limit before meeting with the ad firm. Their job will be to give you the most effective advertising for your money.

2. Recruit a church member with skills in advertising and graphic design who is willing to give his or her time and talents to the church.

3. Create and design your own advertising blitz with the help of several proofreaders and persons with objective opinions.

Ways to Advertise
Local Newspapers
Talk with the advertising department at your local newspaper about size, costs, and deadlines. Ask for help on the layout

if you have not designed a newspaper ad before. You may be able to design the ad on your own computer and take it to the newspaper on disk.

When designing the ad, consider first what is the most important thing you want the reader to see. Then fill in other essential information. Use as few words as possible. If there are too many words, fewer people will read it. White space is important for a clean, easy-to-read ad. Don't clutter it up. If at all possible, design a logo for your service that can be used on all advertisements. Make it contemporary and eye-catching.

A half-page ad can be very effective if designed properly. Remember to include your church's information: address, telephone, Web site address, and an area map. Add a tagline or slogan somewhere in the ad to highlight a positive aspect of your church, such as: "Expect an encounter with the living Christ!" Avoid worn-out clichés and anything controversial. Sincere and welcoming messages will catch the attention of the readers.

Before you develop your ad, ask yourself two questions: "Who is my audience?" and "What message am I trying to convey?" Creating a giant newspaper ad that says, "New Contemporary Worship" will not be effective. The ad needs to describe what contemporary worship is and why this service is the right one for the reader. Why should the reader be interested in your service? People will naturally assume that your ad is a representation of your church. If the ad is noncreative and boring, they will probably assume that your church is boring as well. Image is everything in advertising. If someone doesn't know you, make sure their first impression of you is a good one. Clearly depict who you are in the ad; don't deliver a false message.

Radio Spots

Call your local radio stations to ask about the availability and prices of radio spots (15, 30, or 45 seconds). The station will produce the recording for you. Create the text that you will read for the commercial or have the station use a professional voice. Have several options for background music in mind before speaking with the advertising manager. This can be a powerful tool if a professional, upbeat ad is produced and prime times on the radio are purchased.

Miscellaneous Signs

You may or may not like the idea of yard signs, but it is another way in which to get the word out to the community. Attractive 18" x 24" all-weather signs can be placed in yards. You may also want to design several signs to place around the outside of your church building. When visitors arrive at your church for the first time, carefully placed, visible signs will help them know where to park and enter the building. Ask a nonmember to look over your church and tell you what he or she cannot find easily. Also, remember to add new signs inside your building for contemporary worship. This is an excellent time to evaluate all the signs in your church. Make sure there are enough clear signs to direct people to classrooms, nursery, restrooms, and so on. Also consider adding signs that say: "Quiet, please. Worship in progress."

Flyers

A small flyer can be especially eye-catching if you have an attractive logo design for the service. You might be able to print the flyer or brochure in-house to save money. Only do this if you have a high-quality copier. No one likes to be handed a "this is the best we could do" flyer. Ask the youth of your church if they would like to hand out the flyers at the mall or put them on cars in the parking lot one Saturday. (You probably won't get a "no" on that one.) Give the flyers to church members on Sunday so they can take them to their place of work on Monday and use them as a tool to invite coworkers.

Also make posters from the flyers to take to places of work and other businesses around town. Always get permission to hang a flyer at work and other places of business.

Direct Mail

Design your own one-page, 8" x 11", tri-fold letter. Begin with: "Greetings Neighbor!" The body of the letter should be short and appealing to the eye. Make sure all the pertinent information is covered. Include a small map to your church. Contact your local post office about these types of mailings. You will have to decide to which zip codes you will send the mailings.

There are companies that produce attractive 6" x 9" post-cards, which can be personalized with your message. These will look more professional and will be a little more expensive, but are very effective. Many churches have used these post-cards at Christmas and Easter to advertise special services. You might want to consider using a postcard to advertise your first service.

Local Movie Theaters

Think of all the people who go to the movies. What do they see before the previews and main attraction? Advertising! This is a relatively inexpensive way to get your message out to many people in your community. Check with your local theaters for instructions and prices. Every community is different. Ask if you will be able to make your own ad on slide presentation software and take it to the theater on disk. This will be a savings for your church. It is usually cheaper to sign a contract for six months to one year rather than monthly.

Web Page

Web site advertising is a little different than other types of advertising in that you don't have time or space limitations.

Your page can be an in-depth account of what your church is all about, or what your service is all about. Use this to keep current information available to the Internet-savvy population out there. It's a vastly growing population. Many young to middle-aged people in the workplace have access to the Internet from their office. Most kids have access through school and at home. Use this to communicate to this group of people.

It might be advisable to have your Web site designed professionally. A professional designer is more likely to have the most current tools and technologies at his or her fingertips. Hobbyists rarely have the time to keep current on the methods of Web site designing. If your page isn't current, it will reflect poorly on your service, and might even keep someone from coming to it. Make sure all the information is relevant and easy to find, and most important, that all the information is kept current.

Television

Television advertising is one of the most dramatic and effective types of advertising today. As a society, we are moved by sights and sounds rather than the written and/or printed word. People used to rely on the written word for information and entertainment. Now most people watch television, go to the movies, surf the Web, and take part in other media-rich forms of communication. Society is no longer satisfied unless it moves, shakes, buzzes, and offers to make us rich overnight. Instant gratification is the driving force behind this area of "new media." We want the message quickly. We don't want to have to think about it too much—we want our minds made up for us by a celebrity spokesperson.

The same can be applied to church advertising. Begin by looking at the most popular television shows. Try to advertise during the shows that are most popular with the groups you are trying to reach. There are many extremely popular shows right now concerning the paranormal, angels, and other spiritual and pseudo-spiritual themes. This isn't just some fluke-our society is really searching for spiritual truth again. The resurgence of the New Age movement and other faith practices that focus on the spiritual realm is evidence of this. If that is what the people are hungering for, why not give it to them? Don't merely copy other shows, but address the themes that make these shows popular. This can really start to break down walls between the church and the many nonbelievers who think the church is an "out-of-touch" dinosaur.

To get started in television advertising, Ginghamsburg Church in Tipp City, Ohio has several excellent ads that you can purchase and tag on your church's information at the end. I recommend that you purchase at least one of their ads to use or to simply examine how an ad should be made. (See Resource List at the end of this chapter for their address.)

CHECKLIST #9: ADVERTISING
- Local newspapers
- Radio spots
- Miscellaneous signs
- Flyers
- Direct mailings
- Movie theaters
- Web page
- Television

RESOURCE LIST

Books
Daniel Benedict and Craig Kenneth Miller. *Contemporary Worship for the Twenty-First Century: Worship or Evangelism?* Nashville: Discipleship Resources, 1995. Call: 1-800-685-4370; Fax: 1-404-442-5114.

Paul B. Brown. *In and for the World: Bringing the Contemporary into Christian Worship.* Philadelphia: Fortress Press, 1992.

Marva J. Dawn. *Reaching Out Without Dumbing Down: A Theology of Worship for the Turn-of-the-Century Culture.* Grand Rapids: Wm. B. Eerdmans Publishing Co., 1995.

Michael Slaughter. *Out on the Edge: A Wake-up Call for Church Leaders on the Edge of the Media Reformation.* Nashville: Abingdon Press, 1998. (CD-ROM included.)

Contemporary Worship: A Sourcebook for Spirited-Traditional, Praise and Seeker Services, ed. Tim and Jan Wright. Nashville: Abingdon Press, 1997.

Internet Resources
The Almost Definitive Contemporary Christian Music Hot Page
www.afn.org

Christian Music Online
www.cmo.com

21st Century Strategies, Inc.
www.easum.com
Provides resources, services, and networks to equip church leaders for ministry in the twenty-first century.

Magazines
Church Business
Published bi-monthly by Virgo Publishing, Inc.
3300 N. Central Ave.
Suite 2500

Phoenix, AZ 85012
Call: 1-602-990-1101
Fax: 1-602-990-0819

Church Sound: Sound Advice for Sound Operators
Belew Sound & Visual, Inc.
Call: 1-800-676-4116
Fax: 1-423-764-4116
E-mail: Belewsound@juno.com
A free newsletter published quarterly with valuable training information for your sound operator.

Digital Video
Call: 1-800-998-0806
Internet: www.dv.com

Modern Liturgy
160 E. Virginia St., #290
San Jose, CA 95112
Call: 1-408-286-8505
Internet: MdrnLitrgy@aol.com
Ten issues published per year by Resource Publications, Inc.

Net Results
5001 Avenue "N"
Lubbock, TX 79412-2993
Call: 1-806-762-8094
For church leadership/vitality ideas and methods.

New Media
Call: 1-415-573-5170
Internet: www.hyperstand.com

Presentations
Call: 1-800-328-4329
Internet: www.presentations.com

Song Discovery
Published by CCM Communications
Call: 1-800-433-0700
Internet: www.songdisc@ccmcom.com
Bi-monthly program that includes a CD with accompanying lead sheets and an issue of *Worship Leader* magazine.

Technologies for Worship Magazine
Call: (905) 830-4300
Fax: (905) 853-5096
E-mail: amip@inforamp.net
Internet: www.tfwm.com
Audio, video, music, computers, broadcasting, lighting, drama.

Worship Leader
Published by CCM Communications
Call: 1-800-286-8099
Internet: www.worshipleader.org
Bi-monthly, one-year subscription.

Your Church: Helping You with the Business of Ministry
Published bi-monthly by *Christianity Today, Inc.*
P.O. Box 901013
Fort Worth, TX 76101
Call: 1-800-632-2738

Telemarketing
Outreach Marketing
Call: 1-800-991-6011
Internet: www.outreachmarketing.com

The Phone Is For You
Church Growth Development International
131 E. Grove Ave.
Orange, CA 92865
Call: 1-714-279-6570

Television
Media Ministry Guidebook by Len Wilson and Connie Pack
Ginghamsburg United Methodist Church
6759 South County Rd. 25-A
Tipp City, Ohio
Call: 1-937-667-1069
Fax: 1-937-667-5677

Ginghamsburg also has several professionally produced television ads that you may purchase and tag on your own church's information.

Chapter 10
A Realistic Budget

Setting a budget that you, the congregation, and the finance committee can all live with might be the most difficult task you will tackle before beginning a new service. First, make a list of your needs. Second, research the costs. Third, compare your list and budgets to the example budgets listed in this chapter. Then present your list to the appropriate people and begin discussion on what is feasible for your church.

Budget #1: $3,600

Mixing console (8 to 12 channels)	700
Equalizer	200
Amplifier	300
Four speakers (two house/two monitors)	800
Four microphones (dynamics)	400
Slide projector	300
Music and resources (tapes, CDs)	300
Altar supplies and room decorations	300
Publicity (newspaper)	300
	$3,600

Budget #2: $5,000

Mixing console (8 to 12 channels)	800
Equalizer	200
Amplifier	300
Four speakers (two house/two monitors)	800
Four microphones	400
Two direct boxes	80
Slide projector with remote	600
Music and resources (tapes, CDs)	400
Altar supplies and room decorations	400
Publicity (newspapers and mailings)	1,000
	$4,980

Budget #3: $10,000

Mixing console (16 to 24 channels)	1,200
Sound processors (equalizer and reverb)	400
Amplifier	500
Six speakers (four house/two monitors)	1,200
Four microphones (dynamic)	400
Two wireless microphones	1,000
Three direct boxes	120
Platforms	1,500
Slide projector, remote, long-throw lens	1,000
Music and resources (tapes, CDs)	500
Altar supplies and room decorations	500
Publicity	1,600
	$9,920

Budget #4: $20,000

Mixing console (24 to 32 channels)	2,000
Sound processors (equalizer and reverb)	400
Amplifier	600
Eight speakers (four house/four monitors)	1,600
Six microphones (dynamic)	600
Two wireless and one lapel microphone	1,500
Four direct boxes	160
Platforms	3,000
Video projector	4,500
Computer	2,000
Music and resources	700
Altar supplies and room decorations	600
Publicity	2,000
	$19,660

Budget #5: $30,000

Sound equipment and microphones	6,500
Sound cabinet	300
Synthesizer/bass guitar/drum upgrade	3,500
Video projector/laptop computer	9,200
Spotlights/wiring	4,300
Curtain backdrop	500
Platform skirts	250
Silk trees	437
Altar supplies	300
Music	500
Misc. resources (tapes/CDs/visual Bible)	500
Publicity (newspaper/radio)	3,200
Signs	500
	$29,987

Your church may already own some of the items listed in these budgets. Be sure that these can be used by the new service without affecting another service or group. Use the money that was budgeted for those items to purchase additional supplies or upgrade existing resources.

Items not included in the above budgets:
- CCLI and MPLC licenses
- Music stands and stand lights (if needed)
- Snake, microphone cords, and other power cords

Additional money could be spent on:
- More lapel microphones (helpful for dramas)
- Add-on mixer (for more channels)
- Kneelers
- Banners
- Video equipment

The ongoing yearly budget should include (all amounts are approximate and will depend on your needs):

1.	New microphone cords	100
2.	Repair of sound equipment	200
3.	Replacement bulbs for projectors	100
4.	Upkeep of instruments	200
5.	Growth in sound system, instruments, and lights	500
6.	New music and resources	200
7.	Altar supplies and room decoration	200
		$1,500

If you truly cannot find the money for any of these budgeted items, it is possible to create a contemporary service simply by how you design it. Do all you can to develop your weekly service around a theme that speaks to our current culture. You can be creative and contemporary without technology. Therefore, do not use the excuse "we don't have the money" to keep you from rethinking your style of worship.

CHECKLIST #10: A REALISTIC BUDGET
- Make a list of what is needed for your service and prioritize.
- Compare that list to the suggested budgets.
- Prioritize a "wish" list.
- Meet with finance committee and set a budget.

Chapter 11
Evaluating the Service

If you want to know how the new service is affecting the congregation, you will need a comprehensive survey of those in attendance. This will be the most accurate way to find out if your goals for this new service have been met. There will be as many different answers as there are surveys filled out, but don't be discouraged, for these answers are your true barometer. After tabulating the answers, look for a common denominator. People will respond from a personal point of view, but all those points make up the corporate worship experience. Look at what the people say you are doing well and be encouraged. Look at what the people say you are not doing well and reconsider your approach to these items.

Take a survey at the end of your first six months of services. You may decide to continue to survey the congregation every six months or once a year. The following is a sample contemporary worship survey adapted from *Come Celebrate! A Guide for Planning Contemporary Worship* by Cathy Townley and Mike Graham (Abingdon Press, 1995).

Contemporary Worship Survey

PLEASE RESPOND—WE NEED YOUR INPUT!

On a scale of 1 to 5, please rate the following elements of the contemporary worship service:

MUSIC   LEAST   MOST

1. How well do you like the music overall?   1   2   3   4   5
Explain: _____

2. Do you find the music easy to sing?   1   2   3   4   5
Explain: _____

3. Do you like the amount of singing in the   1   2   3   4   5
   service?
Explain: _____

SERMON

1. Do you like the rotation of our pastors?   1   2   3   4   5
Explain: _____

2. Are the sermons relevant to your daily life?   1   2   3   4   5
Explain: _____

3. Do you like the use of video clips?   1   2   3   4   5
Explain: _____

BULLETIN

1. Is the bulletin easy to follow?   1   2   3   4   5
Explain: _____

2. Does the bulletin give you enough information? 1   2   3   4   5
Explain: _____

	LEAST			MOST	

OVERALL SERVICE

1. Has your worship experience been positive? 1   2   3   4   5
Explain: _____

2. Would you recommend this service to a friend? 1   2   3   4   5
Explain: _____

3. Would you attend this service at another time? 1   2   3   4   5
Explain: _____

Please check all that apply to you:

_____ Church member

_____ Usually attend the 8:30 A.M. blended service

_____ Usually attend the 11:00 A.M. service

_____ Usually attend the 8:30 A.M. contemporary service

_____ First-time visitor

_____ Have visited more than once

Please fill in the blanks:

1. What did you like best about today's service?

2. What did you like least about today's service?

3. Do you have any other comments or suggestions?

Thank you for helping us meet your needs!

You may also want to use another type of survey for feedback. Ask four to six people to serve as evaluators of the service for several weeks. Design a form with specific things you would like them to evaluate (e.g., overall musical sound, musical presentation, sermon presentation, and so on). First, ask them to respond to the questions privately. Then have a group meeting during the week to hear their responses and to discuss what each observed. If you will do this several times during the year, you will get a better understanding of your congregation, how they worship, and whether you are meeting their needs.

Two questions come to mind as I continue to evaluate worship. Is the worship service helping those attending to build a personal and corporate relationship with God? Is the service reaching out to all God's people? Answering these questions objectively will help you get a clear picture of what you are or are not accomplishing in worship.

CHECKLIST #11: EVALUATING THE SERVICE
- Choose people to be on an evaluation team during the year.
- Design a form for the evaluators to use.
- Design a survey for the congregation to complete at six months and one year.

Chapter 12
Conclusion

I believe that worship is the pursuit of God. Our goal should be to enter into God's presence and to sit at God's feet so that we might learn from our loving Creator.

"It's who you are and the way you live that count before God. Your worship must engage your spirit in the pursuit of truth. That's the kind of people the Father is out looking for: those who are simply and honestly *themselves* before him in their worship. God is sheer being itself—Spirit. Those who worship him must do it out of their very being, their spirits, their true selves, in adoration" (John 4:23-24, *THE MESSAGE*).

Worship is who you are; therefore, it begins on Sunday and continues through the week. Worship is a lifestyle, not merely a form. A form is a means to the end. The end we want to achieve in worship is to build a personal and corporate relationship with God. None of this will be achieved if we get "stuck" in worshiping the form.

Contemporary worship is a form we use to come into God's presence. Traditional worship is also a form we use to come into God's presence. They are both valid forms. The same ends can be achieved in both forms of worship. We should not spend time comparing the different forms, but rejoice in the fact that we can use these forms to bring people to the understanding of who they are in God's image. Remember that what is contemporary today will be tomorrow's traditions. The book of Hebrews celebrates the new covenant in Christ—a covenant not based on dead religious form, but on the eternal Spirit:

"Jesus Christ is the same yesterday and today and forever" (Heb. 13:8 NRSV).

What the contemporary form of worship can do for us is give a modern voice to our Christian rituals and traditions. We can use the language and media of today to communicate the gospel to the people of today. The language and media of tomorrow will change and so should our form. But the journey and the destination will always remain the same.

As we grow in Christ, we are to sing a new song to the Lord. It is my prayer that we will all add "new" songs to all the wonderful "old" songs we already know. This will not change our journey's destination. Instead, we will grow in our understanding of God, which will bring about a change of heart.

May God bless your worship journey so that it truly will become life-changing worship.

Glossary

Amplifier: An amplifier increases the power of an audio signal, so that the signal can drive one or more loudspeakers. In sound systems, the power amplifier is always the final active component in the signal chain, located just before the loudspeakers.

Bidirectional Microphone. A type of microphone that is most sensitive to sounds coming from the front or rear of the unit, rejecting sounds from the sides. They are useful where pickup of two separate instruments or voices is desired.

Bus. A line that can connect signals from several sources or destinations. A sound system uses an internal bussing network to route audio signals.

CRT (Cathode Ray Tube). A type of projector that uses three lenses to produce the images (blue, green, and red). It produces the highest picture resolution, but is very expensive and requires permanent installation.

Carbon Microphone. Operates by the movement of a diaphragm that varies the density of pulverized carbon in a small container, resulting in varying resistance to a voltage. Carbon microphones do not have the best sonic characteristics, but are sturdy and inexpensive.

Cardioid Microphone. The cardioid is probably the most popular microphone in terms of pickup patterns. (It is named for the heart-shaped pickup pattern.) It is most sensitive to sounds coming in on the primary axis, rejecting sounds from the sides and rear. This helps to reduce feedback and increase system gain.

Compressor. An electronic device that adjusts the volume of a microphone up and down, depending on whether a speaker is whispering or shouting. This device is useful in contemporary worship services, in which speakers have varying styles of delivery.

Condenser Microphone. A condenser microphone used a gold-coated plastic diaphragm, mounted above a conductive back plate. When the diaphragm vibrates in response to sound, the electrical charge induced in the back plate generates a fluctuating voltage to represent the original sound wave. Condensers have excellent sound quality and are widely used in recording.

Contact Pickup Microphone. Contact pickups are microphone elements that detect sound waves in a solid substance, rather than in air. They are used almost exclusively for instruments. Critically placed using sticky wax, they pick up sound directly from the body of the instrument, such as a guitar. They are resistant to feedback, but rarely produce a true sound quality, so they are not often used in recording.

DAT (Digital Audio Tape). A specific stereo cassette format using rotating heads to record and play back tracks as a series of angled stripes, rather than continuous linear tracks. Sampled sounds are recorded in rapid succession, translated into numbers, then retranslated and played back in the proper order and at the proper speed to recreate the original sound. Sound can be duplicated over and over with no reduction in fidelity (no tape "hiss").

Decibel (dB). A unit of sound wave measurement that compares the strength of one sound to another. The basic unit, a *Bel*, represents a ratio between two power levels, rather than an absolute value. This unit, divided into tenths, is a decibel. The reference point for decibels is usually the threshold of hearing, or the softest sound audible to humans.

DLP (Digital Light Processing). A type of projector that uses tiny mirrors to reflect and focus light through a lens onto a screen. Produces high resolution and varying brightness levels.

De-Esser. A type of signal processor that momentarily compresses high signal levels (6 kHz to 8 kHz range) to control the effects of sibilance (when sibilant consonants, such as S's and T's, are too prominent in singing and speaking).

Diaphragm Microphone. The diaphragm in a microphone is a thin, flexible disk that is connected to a coil of fine wire, which is mounted in a magnetic gap so it can move freely within the gap. Sound waves cause the diaphragm to vibrate, generating an electrical current.

Direct Box. A specially designed signal transformer that converts the high-impedance signal from the instrument to a low-impedance signal for the mixing console. Direct boxes also prevent the instrument from picking up phantom-power voltages (wireless microphones), and help to eliminate the "hum" that can be picked up between audio units.

Dynamic Microphone. The dynamic microphone operates by the action of a diaphragm, which vibrates in response to sound, causing the coil to create an electrical current. The current is the electrical representation of the original sound wave. Dynamic microphones are dependable, rugged, and insensitive to environmental factors, which make them a good choice for outdoor use.

Echo Bus. In a mixing console, the echo bus (also called effects or auxiliary) incorporates external signal processing into the mix. The term *echo* refers to its primary use—to add electronic reverb or delay to the sound).

Electret Condenser Microphone. Electrets are a special class of condenser microphones. They use diaphragms made of a type of plastic that retains a static charge indefinitely. They require a built-in amplifier powered by a battery housed in the microphone case. They can be made very small, and can be used for close-miking techniques.

Equalizer. A device that evens out ("equalizes") the frequency spectrum, balancing the lows, middles, and highs. Turning up the bass tone control, for example, increases the level of lower frequency sounds, resulting in a richer, fuller sound. Turning the bass down results in a thinner sound. Some situations require the sound to be unequal, for example, when a voice or sound needs to stand out among others. Types of equalizers include: multi-band, parametric, graphic, and digital.

Feedback. Undesirable noise that occurs when the sound picked up by a microphone is reproduced by a loudspeaker and *fed back* into the sound system repeatedly. This howling or squealing sound can reach overpowering levels.

Filter. A device used in signal processing that allows some frequencies to pass through the system, while blocking others. There are high-pass (*passes* frequencies above its cutoff point) and low-pass (*weakens* frequencies above its cutoff point) filters.

Flanging. A special effect used in signal processing to produce sounds ranging from hollow or metallic to a "whooshing" noise.

Gigabyte (gig). Refers to units of measure used for computer memory. A gigabyte equals approximately one thousand megabytes.

Hand-held Microphone. The most common type of microphone for speakers and singers, it is well-insulated to prevent handling noise and for protection if it is dropped. It can also be mounted on a stand.

Hemispherical Microphone. Referring to the microphone's pickup pattern, the hemispherical is a pressure response type. When placed on a boundary surface, such as a table, the microphone picks up sound from all directions in front of (above) the surface, but does not pick up sound behind (below) the surface.

Hertz (Hz). A unit of measurement that indicates sound wave frequency in cycles per second. Generally, the higher the frequency, the higher the perceived pitch of the sound.

High-impedance. Refers to microphone output impedance (measured in *ohms*), high-impedance units include piezoelectric contact pickups, guitar pickups, and inexpensive microphones. High-impedance microphones are limited to cables about twenty feet long.

Hypercardioid Microphone. Hypercardioid refers to a highly directional microphone element. It offers a concentrated forward pickup lobe (greater rejection of sounds coming in from the sides and rear).

LCD (Liquid Crystal Display). A single lens projector that offers portability and is cost-effective. Some models come with built-in speakers and extra inputs and outputs to allow for connection with other video sources. Low-priced models may cause some visible pixelization (see **pixel/pixelization**).

Lavalier Microphone. A lavalier microphone is a small element designed to clip directly to clothing (also referred to as a lapel microphone). Modern lavaliers are almost always the electret type, which can be made very small, offer good high-frequency response, and are reasonable in price.

Low-impedance. Refers to the output of a microphone, low-impedance units are less susceptible to extraneous noise pickup in the cable. They can drive cables hundreds of feet long. Most professional microphones are low-impedance and are preferred in live sound reinforcement and recording settings.

Megabyte (meg). A unit of computer information storage. A megabyte equals approximately one million bytes.

Microphone. A device that picks up sound vibrations and converts them into electrical energy (the audio signal) by using a diaphragm. A microphone is a type of transducer, a device that converts energy from one form into another.

MIDI (Musical Instrument Digital Interface). A hardware standard by which different electronic devices (such as a computer and a musical instrument) can be connected to allow information to be transmitted and received.

Mixer. A small unit with four to twelve input channels that is used by live performing groups. The mixer combines and reroutes audio signals from a set of signal input channels to a set of signal output channels to modify the signal through sound enhancement circuitry. Larger units with more channels are referred to as mixing consoles.

Noise Gates. A signal processor that turns off or weakens the audio signal passing through it when the signal level falls below an adjustable threshold. This will mute low-level hiss and noise, or leakage from other sound sources. Noise gates can be used for automatically muting microphones that are temporarily not being used during a service.

Omnidirectional Microphone. Omnidirectional refers to a type of pickup pattern—the way in which the element responds to sounds that come in from different directions. Omnidirectional elements pick up sound equally from all directions. Generally, this results in feedback problems, but omnidirectionals have a good low-frequency response and are not susceptible to breath and wind noises.

Parabolic Microphone. The parabolic microphone is a conventional element connected to a reflector that concentrates sound on the element. Highly directional and sensitive, parabolic units are used in outdoor recording settings primarily.

Piezoelectric Microphone. The diaphragm in a piezoelectric microphone is connected to a crystal element. The crystal is a material that is physically deformed by pressure to generate a voltage. These microphones are not of high sound quality, but are inexpensive. They are easily damaged and sensitive to heat and humidity.

Pixel/Pixelization. Pixels are small discrete elements (visible dots) that together constitute an image (as on a television screen). High-resolution projection systems have a higher pixel number (the number of pixels or dots on the screen), which reduces the pixelization effect.

Presbycusis. The technical term for loss of hearing sensitivity due to aging. This involves difficulty in hearing higher frequencies and some degradation of speech intelligibility. Loss of hearing is also a problem among those who are continually exposed to ear-damaging environments, such as rock concerts, construction sites, and factory settings.

Pressure Response Microphone. Also called a "boundary" microphone, the technology is relatively new and subject to patent and trademark restrictions. The unit is placed close to a flat plate, picking up pressure variations in the air gap between the element and the plate. Developed for recording, the pressure response principle offers a hemispherical pickup pattern with some feedback problems.

Ribbon Microphone. The method of transduction is similar to that used in dynamic microphones. A very thin, corrugated metal ribbon is stretched inside the air gap of a magnet. The ribbon vibrates in response to sound, creating a very small voltage. All ribbon microphones require a built-in transformer, which boosts the signal voltage.

Shotgun Microphone. The shotgun microphone is a highly directional unit, most often used in broadcasting and film production. They are rarely used in live sound reinforcement.

Signal Processor. A device that alters the character of the sound, such as frequency spectrum (equalizers and filters); volume (compressors, limiters, and noise gates); or spaciousness (reverb and delay). Signal processors are inserted between various audio units depending on where the sound will be modified.

Stand-mounted Microphone. A microphone that is specifically designed to be mounted on a stand. These are usually made for recording purposes where isolation from shock and external vibration is possible.

Supercardioid Microphone. Supercardioid refers to a highly directional microphone element. It supplies less rejection of sounds coming from the rear than the cardioid. The forward pickup lobe is more concentrated, offering greater rejection of sounds coming in from the sides.

Wireless microphones. A wireless microphone system uses miniaturized components similar to a commercial FM broadcasting system. The transmitter fits into the microphone handle. Both the microphone and the transmitter are battery-operated, freeing the user to move around while speaking, singing, or playing an instrument. The transmitted sound is picked up by a receiver that is wired to the amplifier and the loudspeakers.